RUNNING FROM THE SHADOWS

Stephanie Hickey lives in County Waterford with her partner of sixteen years. She has four children and runs most days in the valleys of the townlands where she grew up. She ran a half-marathon six months after taking up running and she has never looked back.

Shane Dunphy worked for fifteen years as a frontline child protection worker in many different parts of Ireland. He now teaches social studies and psychology and is a regular contributor to television and radio programmes on issues of child and family welfare. He is the author of several non-fiction books, including *Wednesday's Child* and *The Boy They Tried to Hide*. He is also the author of the David Dunnigan crime thriller series, writing under the name S.A. Dunphy.

RUNNING FROM THE SHADOWS

A true story of childhood abuse and how one
woman faced her past, and ran towards her future

STEPHANIE HICKEY
with
Shane Dunphy

HACHETTE
BOOKS
IRELAND

First published in Ireland in 2020 by
HACHETTE BOOKS IRELAND

1

Cataloguing in Publication Data is available from the British Library

Trade paperback ISBN 9781529327182
Ebook ISBN 9781529327199

Typeset in Cambria by Bookends Publishing Services, Dublin

Printed and bound in Great Britain by Clays Ltd, Elcograf, S.p.A

Hachette Books Ireland policy is to use papers that are natural, renewable and
recyclable products and made from wood grown in sustainable forests. The logging
and manufacturing processes are expected to conform to the environmental
regulations of the country of origin.

Hachette Books Ireland
8 Castlecourt Centre
Castleknock
Dublin 15, Ireland

A division of Hachette UK Ltd
Carmelite House, 50 Victoria Embankment, EC4Y 0DZ
www.hachettebooksireland.ie

For Angelo, Danielle, Philip, Dylan and Riccardo

Some names and details within this book have been
changed to respect the privacy of individuals

Foreword

Shane Dunphy, Waterford, July 2019

I have been writing about child protection and the resilience of the human spirit for more than a decade. Because I am moderately well known for this, I am contacted on an almost weekly basis by people wanting me to help them write their stories.

In the main, I respond with a gentle 'no'.

I am not a professional ghost writer, and I always worry that the process of reliving such traumatic experiences may prove more damaging than healing. I have also read what some in the publishing world refer to as 'misery memoirs' that were highly exploitative, and I have never been in the business of voyeurism or pornography.

In some instances I have recommended ghost writers whose work I respect, but until Stephanie Hickey crossed my path, I have never been tempted to write such a book myself.

So what made me change my mind?

In the days approaching the Christmas of 2018 I was contacted by a lady called Claire Bridle. Claire is a book blogger whose work I greatly admire, and she asked me if I was aware of a recent case that had just concluded in the Central Criminal Court. I had read about Stephanie and Deedee in the papers, and I knew that for an Irish court to hand down a sentence of ten years for a case of historic sexual abuse, there must have been pretty damning evidence. Claire explained that she was a friend of Stephanie's and that Ms Hickey was interested in writing a book about her experiences bringing the case to trial.

She wanted to tell the story of just how challenging it is for an ordinary person to find themselves within the legal system, and how that system treats you once you are caught in its grip.

This immediately interested me. The idea of exploring what it is like for someone already experiencing trauma to have to live that pain while in the belly of a vast, bureaucratic system is something I have tried to write about in other books, but always from the perspective of an insider looking out. Here was a chance to speak to someone who had navigated that system from its figurative source to the ocean.

I was intrigued to meet Stephanie and discuss her experiences, but I still couldn't see myself writing the book. I thought our conversation might make an interesting feature piece for one of the newspapers I occasionally write for, and I decided, as in every other case, that I would say 'no thanks' and pass Stephanie on to someone else.

But then I met her, and everything changed.

Stephanie is a tall, slim woman with the build of an

athlete. She has a profoundly intelligent face and piercing eyes, and when we met in Geoff's pub in Waterford City one Friday afternoon in December, I was immediately struck by her courage. This was a lady who had been through an incredible ordeal, but who had not let it beat her. Her conversation, even when talking about very difficult things that day, was infused with humour and self-awareness. Survivors of abuse often develop a funereally dark sense of the absurd, and Stephanie had that in spades.

In the space of about an hour she spoke about her experiences, but she also spoke about music and faith and wild birds and foxes and the beautiful sound of a pub filled to bursting just before closing time.

And I loved the way she spoke.

As a writer, language is my business. Stephanie speaks with the rhythm, musicality and lilt of the Nire Valley, and as she told me about her world, I found myself living it right along with her. It is fair to say that Stephanie Hickey wooed me with her remarkable ability to communicate, and she did it without even knowing. The cadence of her articulation excited me, and I found myself wishing I had brought a notebook to our meeting – I wanted to write down some of her phrases there and then. By the time I left the pub that afternoon, I knew I wanted to help her share those experiences with the world.

But of course, a book needs a publisher, and we didn't have one.

My editor at Hachette Ireland immediately expressed

an interest, and in the spring of 2019, Stephanie and I sat down in a beautiful house she had rented in the middle of the Nire Valley and over two days I recorded twelve hours of conversation.

I was worried about this process, perhaps more than I let on to Stephanie at the time. Years of working with children and adults who have experienced abuse have taught me how exhausting it can be to have to relive those awful moments.

My friend and fellow author Sue Leonard was invaluable in giving me some guidance on how to structure and frame each day, and how much material I was likely to need. I had visions of recording weeks' worth of conversation, but Sue (an experienced ghost writer) assured me that this would cause more problems than it would solve, and that less was more.

So with Sue's sage advice ringing in my ears, I planned out our days very carefully. First thing in the morning, when we were well rested and full of caffeine, we tackled the dark material; around lunchtime we covered the court case and the legal stuff, and as the afternoon turned to evening we turned to happier times – childhood memories, opinions about the world, observations on survival.

I want to pay tribute to Stephanie here – never for one moment did she dry up or even ask to take a break. I pressed 'record' and we would begin.

We huddled around the fire, drank tea and she talked and I listened, asking the occasional question – but mostly,

Stephanie simply told her story. She brought me back to her days growing up in Touraneena, she took me on drives in that van with Batty and we visited the house in Tallow where so many dark and frightening things occurred. I learned about the songs her father sang and I sat beside her in her local church on the day she got married. Time and again I stood eye to eye with Bartholomew Prendergast, the monster that hides in the shadows of Stephanie's life, and saw him as she did.

And, of course, she took me running. Rarely have I heard someone speak so eloquently and passionately about their sport, and it did not take me long to realise this would be a major part of the story we were going to tell.

On the second and final day her whole family came over and we shared a meal.

I appreciated this more than I can express because I was beginning to feel like a tourist in her world – the embrace of this amazing group of people reassured me that I had been accepted. They were giving me their blessing.

But this is Stephanie's tale. I don't want to offer my analysis or tell you what she is trying to say – I'll let you decide that for yourself.

I do think it is worth mentioning something she said during the last conversation we had, though. Time and again during our recordings, Stephanie would speak about how she hoped her story would help others going through the same experiences: children or young people or adults who have been made feel alone and isolated by someone in a position of power or authority. Stephanie wanted them to know they are not alone, and that it is possible to come out the other end. To not just survive, but to thrive. She sincerely hoped some parts of her story would resonate.

I asked her what she felt she had learned from all of this.

'To not be afraid,' she said without pausing. 'When things were at their most awful and I thought life was unbearable, I would go for a run and see the sun rise and be struck by how beautiful it was. Or I would switch on the radio and a song would come on and a line of the lyrics would make me feel better. Or one of my kids would say something funny and I would laugh, and it's hard to be miserable when you're laughing. Or Angelo would just be there, like he always is, through thick and thin. When it all seemed too much I would think about these things, and I wouldn't be scared any more.'

Stephanie has looked into the darkness but did not let what she saw there overwhelm her.

She fought her monsters and won.

This book is her way of saying that you can, too.

I feel privileged to have shared a small part of the journey with her.

DUBLIN

AUGUST 2018

Caught in a Strange Loop

I'm forty-six years old, and today I'm running because I need to, maybe more than I've ever needed to before.

It's weird because I can feel all the familiar, comfortable sensations I always experience when I enact this physical ritual: the peace, the warmth that seems to radiate from all of my muscles, the joy that starts as a tiny flame deep inside and gradually burns right through me – all are present, but this time I have a nagging sense of being in a dream.

And it's not a good one.

I look across, and my older sister, Deirdre (who is always known affectionately as Deedee) is running beside me. I'm glad she's here. I can see the same aura of unreality on her face too, but she's keeping pace and there's three kilometres left to go and, for now, we're safe and the world can't reach us.

Maybe that's what running does for me more than anything else: it offers an escape. And I've never needed to escape more than I do now.

We've been staying in the Liffey Valley Hotel, just off the M50 motorway, for the past couple of days. The first day we sat in our room or went to the café. We talked about everything that had happened and all the things we were afraid might still happen. I don't know if the talking did any good, but it was as if we just needed to get it all out. I can't remember a lot of what we said, but I do know there were things we shared that we hadn't before. It felt good and it felt terrible and we laughed and cried a lot.

Maybe it was all the big, difficult emotions, but the hotel room started to seem too small, and we began to feel pent up and trapped and needed to move. We swam in the pool a few times, but then, virtually simultaneously, we decided it was time to run. One of the lifeguards told us about a 5K loop – a circular track that would lead us safely back to the hotel – that goes over the motorway, past the shopping centre and around some housing estates. Thrilled by this knowledge, we put on our gear and struck out.

And here we are.

One of the strangest things for me is running in a place without trees, mostly on the flat. Where I live, in the Nire Valley in west Waterford, it's all mountains and hills, it's green, and as I run all I can hear is the wind through the branches and the call and answer of birds. But here, right in the middle of the commuter belt, the ambient noise is car engines and the bleat of horns and people shouting to one another in accents that I mostly hear on the TV.

But I'm running and that means I'm in a bubble and all of that is on the outside and it can't get to me. The beauty of running is that it's so simple: it's about being in motion – you put one foot in front of the other and you keep doing that until you get to the finish line.

Sometimes it seems to me that's what my life has been about.

It hasn't always been clear to me where the finishing line was, but I knew I needed to stay in motion. Running gives your days a rhythm – the pounding of your feet on the ground and the beating of your heart create a drum track that anchors you, and I know for the first time, as Deedee and I complete that first strange Dublin loop, that this is what I have been searching for for so many years. The search brought me to some scary places, but it was worth it.

We reach the sliding doors of the hotel and stop to do some stretching. I feel loose and full of oxygen, as if my veins have opened up wide and the blood is pumping freely and easily. After a run, it's always like I can accomplish anything – nothing seems too great a challenge.

But then, as if it has been hovering above me in a big black cloud, I remember why Deedee and I are in Dublin in the first place, and the nerves and the anxiety and the anger come crashing back.

My big sister and I are here to face down the man who ruined our lives – the man who abused us and took away our childhoods.

In a couple of days' time, we'll be walking into the Central Criminal Court to do battle with a monster, and I just hope we have the strength.

The monster's name is Bartholomew Prendergast and he is my brother-in-law.

On the Defensive

The Central Criminal Court looks just like you'd expect it to, the same as courtrooms look on television or in the movies. It's a big, airy room, all wood panels, and the floor is covered in red carpet tiles. You probably think it's strange I would notice something like the colour of the carpet, but my mind is having all sorts of conversations with itself and doing all kinds of bizarre things as I sit in this space, somewhere I never in a million years thought I'd be.

I feel like I'm watching everything happen from somewhere else. The silence in the courtroom is eerie, like they've sucked all the sound out of it, or maybe that my head has been filled up with cotton wool and all the noise you normally experience has been muffled.

The platform where the judge is going to be sitting seems impossibly high, yet at the same time I have a flight of fancy that I could reach out and touch that empty chair without even moving from my seat. The perspective is all wrong – things seem madly far away but also crushingly close.

My eyes roll involuntarily to the left, and I see him.

Bartholomew – I always called him Batty, although the name leaves a foul taste in my mouth now, like it's inappropriately familiar – is sitting with his legal team. He's sixty-six years old now, and he looks it – I've never noticed before, but today, as if a veil has been lifted, I can see the bags under his eyes, the deep lines on his face, the grey pallor to his skin. It is as if the darkness inside him is forcing its way out. He is dressed in a casual jacket, a shirt and jeans and in his hand is a blue-and-white plastic shopping bag.

My mind fixes on the bag. It seems so out of place and odd – this man, who altered the path of my life irreparably, is clutching this cheap, flimsy bag as if it is a talisman. I wonder if he has a jumper in it, or maybe some medication, or even a snack. Why didn't his barrister tell him to leave it outside? I try to push the thought process aside and refocus on the task at hand, but my eyes are drawn back to him. I suddenly realise that he hasn't looked at me once since the police led him in. I hope he's ashamed.

He seems so calm, so undisturbed, while I'm sick to my stomach and my head won't slow down.

All my life Batty has been a huge character – even though he is of average size, he always seemed to be a massively big man, dressed in the height of fashion, his blond hair worn long, his face rarely without a smile. While he worked for the council as a lorry driver, he was a local celebrity in our little area of west Waterford, playing in a well-known pub band.

Batty was the life and soul of the party.

When he came into my family's orbit, he charmed all of us. My parents, particularly my mother, adored him. When we heard he was going to marry my sister Patricia, we were all over the moon.

You see, we thought we knew the sort of man he was – kind of full of himself, a little brash and a bit loud, but a decent man, despite those small faults.

But we didn't know him at all. We hadn't a clue there was a darkness in him, a sickness. Today, the world will learn who Batty Prendergast really is.

This is my second time here – a few days earlier, the whole family gathered, thinking the ordeal we hoped might end this sorry, sordid, painful part of our lives was actually going to be done with, but the case was adjourned.

I was devastated. I'd told myself that, as dreadful as I knew the whole thing would be, this was my day, this was my chance. I'd prepared for it mentally. I had taken the frightened, injured teenager that always sits just at the edge of my being and tucked her away so that all the world would see a confident, strong woman. That woman is a mask I put on, but I knew I would need her.

I was ready. I felt, come what may, I could do it.

That first day I looked down from the windows of the

green room, where families and victims are kept while waiting for their cases to be heard, and saw all the people coming and going outside the court, and even though they didn't know I was there and they were all wrapped up in their own troubles and concerns, it seemed to me that they must all somehow be aware of my case and the reason I was in the building on that day.

I was convinced they would look up and point and say: 'There's Stephanie, the woman who was molested and raped by her brother-in-law and who still let the bastard take the photographs at her wedding.'

After all the years, a part of me – just a small part, but the voice still makes itself heard – feels the shame of it. It's shame I don't deserve and I don't need in my life, but it squirms its way into my head and it takes every grain of energy to push it aside.

That first day I sat in this same room, with my partner, Angelo, and my children, Dylan, who is nineteen, Philip who is twenty-four, and Danielle who is twenty-five, and I listened as the judge read through my statement, outlining each specific count against Batty. I felt as if these were my crimes, as if I was the one on trial. My knees shook, I was terrified I would have a panic attack, and the whole thing seemed to go on forever.

I had been warned by my court liaison officer, Clare, when I first met her three years ago, that this would be a long and hard road. She's been with me every step of the way, but it still came as a shock to hear the charges read out. I was so relieved when it finished, but that was when the real bombshell was dropped: Batty's team had lodged an application to have all the cases heard separately. This meant that my abuse case and that of my sister would be heard individually, on different days, and this usually means much more lenient sentencing. I was furious, but there was nothing I could do about it.

The judge said he wanted to take a few days to consider this and he would come back with his decision at that stage, which was why Deirdre and I had decided to stay in Dublin.

Now I'm back.

The judge comes in, but it's not the same one – this time it's a woman, Justice Eileen Creedon. She is pleasant-looking, I'm guessing a similar age to myself, but her taking over the case means I have to sit through the whole process of hearing the counts against Batty again – so all the details are read into the record anew. I know I should be used to it by now, but I feel as wretched as I did on the first day. I put my head down and try to control my breathing and pray I won't faint.

Finally, it's over and there is all sorts of discussion and debate around the judge's bench that I can't really hear. I know they're talking about my case, but it is clear that this is not meant for me to participate in, or even to understand, which makes me feel even more like an outsider, as if these are great minds discussing my fate and that I will be informed when their deliberations are complete. This goes on for a long time, and just when I think something might happen, we are informed that court is breaking for lunch.

I think I might scream. Tears start to roll down my cheeks, and I have to hang onto the bench in front of me. Just before she leaves her podium, Justice Creedon peers down at us and announces that she has decided not to hear the cases separately – they will be heard together. With that, she whisks out.

I stand there, suddenly realising what has happened.

I've won the first battle.

I glance over, and the great Bartholomew Prendergast doesn't look quite so confident any more. For the first time since I decided to press charges against the man who almost destroyed me, I feel a sense of hope.

THE NIRE VALLEY, WATERFORD

THE 1980S

The Borrow

The wild, hilly, mountainous regions of west Waterford are in my heart and soul. It's only when I'm away from them for any length of time that I understand just how important they are to me, because I miss them terribly.

I'm not sure what it is: the gentle rolling undulation of the roads and pathways, built to the rise and fall of the rugged landscape, seems to comfort me. Or maybe it's the musical, lilting rhythm of the speech, which makes every conversation like a kind of song. I walk outside my back door to hang out washing or just to take in the air, and I'm likely to see a fox or a badger wander across my garden – they throw me a casual glance as if to say 'hello, neighbour'. When I drive into the village to buy some milk or to pick up a loaf of bread, I will know each and every person I pass on the narrow roads by name, and they'll all wave as they go past.

The trees have a distinct shade of green and the rocks have a blue-grey hue like nowhere else. This is where I belong and I am in no doubt of it. I never want to live anywhere else. I can run around my area and trace my early life and the history of my family, as the landmarks and archaeology of it are still there for all to see.

I was born in 1971 in a small two-bedroomed cottage in the townland of Clonegegaile just outside the village of Touraneena in west Waterford. Touraneena lies in a kind of valley that makes up the Sliabh na gCua district, which sits right between the Comeraghs and the Knockmealdown mountains. People called the area the cottage was situated in The Borrow – I'm not sure why.

My early childhood was full of friends, family and music.

I was the youngest in the family, with fourteen years between my eldest brother and me, but despite the wide spread of ages, we were a close-knit bunch, and my earliest memories are of wandering the lanes and fields around our home, picking berries, playing hide-and-seek and visiting neighbours. It was the kind of childhood that really doesn't exist any more – back then no one worried if children weren't seen from sun-up until dusk, and we always went around in packs, so I suppose there was less cause for worry.

And I discovered, anyway, the danger was inside our home, not outside it.

My mother, Kathleen, was a strong, warm-hearted, powerful woman who was a real homemaker. In the house in The Borrow there was no washing machine, no inside toilet, and it was quite crowded, but my memory is that she was always there and the house was always filled with the smell of her baking – butterfly buns and pineapple cake and Victoria sponge were always on the table, like an expression of love made from flour and butter and jam. My mother was always there – I don't remember ever coming home to an empty house. Her presence seemed to give the cottage its own kind of security and identity.

My father's name was Tommy Hickey. He was a well-known singer, accordion player and set-dancer. People would come from far and wide to our house to hear him singing, and his family had a history of republicanism – he grew up in an IRA safe-house and de Valera stayed there during the War of Independence. My father was an all-Ireland champion dancer, and he taught all of us to sing and dance, too.

I remember him sitting in our kitchen at home, and he would pick up two spoons and strike up a rhythm with them, singing or sometimes whistling a tune (what the old musicians call 'lilting' or 'gob music'), and he would get us to dance. He could literally make music and create a tune from nothing.

He had a huge reverence for the writing of a Waterford man called Pádraig Ó Miléadha, and his favourite song was 'The Little Village Schoolroom of Kilbrien', which is another village just beyond Touraneena. My father had a fantastic voice, and people would always ask him to sing this:

It is twenty years or more since I left my native shore
To seek an exiled life across the foam.
But the friends I left behind are still fresh within my mind
And I never can forget my dear old home.

In my dreams I worship still in the old church on the hill
Where my hands in Sunday prayer I used to join.
And my memory flies each day o'er the ocean far away
To the little village schoolroom of Kilbrien.

When I listen back to that song now, I can see that my father was very similar to me in that he had a deep love of where he was from – Pádraig Ó Miléadha's song is steeped in a longing for home.

When I was seven, we moved, lock, stock and barrel, to a much bigger house in Touraneena, about five miles away. I was delighted to have more space and to have friends closer by, but a big part of me missed that little cottage in The Borrow, and still does. I often run past it and it always fills me with a sense of happiness and freedom.

It was in this new home in Touraneena that Bartholomew Prendergast first visited us. I don't remember the first time I saw him – I know I was about nine years old – but it's almost like he was always there, just waiting for his chance to strike.

A Musical Interlude

I'm nine years old.

There is a fiftieth birthday party in Dunford's pub in Touraneena – it's for one of our neighbours, the Quinlans, and the whole village has turned out. I'm not supposed to be in a pub at eight o'clock at night (I'm far too young), but no one seems to mind, and I sit in the corner sandwiched between my mother and my older brother Richard, loving every minute of the festivities unfolding before me. I've been told to stay quiet and not give anyone a reason to notice I'm there, and I'm doing my best to do just that, but it's tough with so much going on and so many interesting things to see.

The place is packed to the rafters. The crowd is a

patchwork of bright, grinning faces flushed with alcohol, ties askew and hair awry. I catch snatches of conversation and brays of laughter. My mother is leaning across the table talking to Bridgie from Dungarvan. I listen in to their chatter for a while, but I soon get bored and let my mind drift. The air is thick with tobacco smoke and the smell of stale beer, and music booms from a tiny stage against the far wall.

It's music like I've never come across before.

Three men are on the stage. The lead singer is wearing a tight T-shirt with the sleeves roughly cut off so it looks almost like a vest. His high-waisted stone-washed jeans are so tight they seem virtually sprayed to his legs, and he has a red electric guitar slung low about his waist. Beside him is a man I know to be his brother, playing bass, and behind them a guy on drums. The band is called Stardust and I am captivated by the sound they are making.

I have been brought up in a house where music is a constant presence, but this is something else entirely – it is so loud I can feel my eardrums vibrate, and instead of the respectful silence that usually greets my father's songs, the partygoers in Dunford's are all singing along – bellowing along, really – and punching the air in time to the chorus of 'Sweet Caroline...'

The singer is drenched in sweat, his long blond locks plastered back on his head, dark patches of perspiration soaking through the lime green of his top, making dark rings around his armpits. He plays a low melody on the bass strings of the guitar and most of the people sing along to this part as well: *'Dah-dah-dum, da-da-da-da-dum, da-da-dum!'* He wiggles his hips and points the head of the guitar at the crowd, as if he is shooting the notes at them.

He has them in the palm of his hands.

His name is Batty Prendergast, and he has just started going out with my sister Patricia, who is twenty-one.

My dad appears through the swarm of people and leaves a glass of orange and a packet of crisps on the table for me and a glass of Guinness for Mammy. He leans in and tells my mother that they should probably be getting me home soon. It's so loud I can barely hear him, but I get the gist of what he's saying.

'One more song!' I beg.

He smiles and ruffles my hair and grins – he always finds it hard to say no to me, and I am not beyond playing up on it.

'I'll be back over here in half an hour and you'd better be ready to go then, d'ye hear me?'

I grin and nod my head vigorously, knowing he'll forget and it'll be hours before I'm sent back to the house. 'Sweet Caroline' comes to an end, and without pausing for a second Batty plays the opening chords to 'Jailhouse Rock'. The pub goes wild. Even though he looks nothing like Elvis, somehow my sister's new boyfriend manages to do a more than passable impression, and before I know it I'm standing up on the seat, dancing along and singing the bits of the song I know.

Through the crowd, I can see Tisha (which is what we all

call Patricia) sitting on a barstool gazing at the stage with love-struck eyes. I think she's dreadfully silly to go all gooey over a fella, but even I have to admit, this one is something of a catch.

Everyone in Touraneena knows Batty Prendergast. He's a star – at least he is in our world, anyway.

As he finishes the Elvis number with a flourish of his red guitar, Batty looks over at me and winks. I wish I could say it makes me uncomfortable or frightens me or gives me the creeps, but it doesn't.

I'm just a kid at a party in a pub, with my family and friends all around me.

What is there to be afraid of?

A West Waterford Childhood

The world of my youth is a place of no mobile phones and no social media. It seems a quiet, safe, friendly place. The universe is the homestead (our house in Touraneena had once been the schoolhouse, and I always have the feeling I am walking on layers of history), the parish church, the fields, woods, hills and boreens of the Nire, and the small local school three minutes' walk from my front door.

That front door is always left open, and anyone who calls is immediately fed – they aren't even asked if they are hungry, my mother just assumes (which, in rural Ireland in the 1980s, is probably a fair guess) and a plate of food is put in front of them, along with a mug of strong tea. My mother considers it simply unacceptable to allow anyone to leave our house with an empty belly.

A wise person once said that it takes a village to raise a child, and there is great truth in those words. My parents grew up a hundred yards from one another, and in Touraneena I have a group of friends I love dearly within a thirty-second walk from my house. Deirdre, Siobhan, Shane, Triona, Ailish, Cathal – we share long sunlit days of summer and cracklingly cold mountain winters. Together we navigate the highs and lows and victories and defeats of moving towards adolescence.

Sport is a constant presence – there is always football and hurling, but we like the more exotic foreign sports too. When Wimbledon plays out its starched white splendour on the black-and-white television in our living room, Deirdre and I go to the tarmacadamed space behind the school and knock a handball back and forth – I am Chris Evert and she is Martina Navratilova.

On bicycles that are not built for such terrain, we range far and wide, pretending to be the Famous Five, convinced we will find a secret passage leading to buried treasure deep below the mountains. We never find it, but we have fun looking.

When the blackberries are in season we are gone from early morning until late. It is a race to see who can get to the most heavily laden bushes, and we fill buckets and lug them back to the shed behind my house. I like to go out early some mornings and breathe in the heady scent as the berries start to ferment – it reminds me of the smell in the pub.

Every two or three weeks a man comes from Ardfinnan and pays us for the berries according to their weight – he uses them to make black dye. He has a huge old scales on the back of his lorry, and the buckets are hung from a hook and he calculates the price on an old scrap of paper with the stub of a pencil. A couple of well-filled containers could earn you as much as two or three old pounds, which is a fortune to us.

The other thing I love is farming. My Auntie Cissy never married, so she dotes on her nieces and nephews. She still lives in my mother's home place in Boolavounteen, and often in the summer months I cycle over and help out with the daily chores. The biggest job is bringing in the hay. We make up cocks of the precious golden strands, which are stacked on a trailer at the back of a tractor, and all the cousins sit up on top of these stacks – it's a great thrill for us, as we're likely to fall off when the tractor takes a corner, but no one ever seems to mind! You end up on your back in a ditch, but you pull yourself out and run after the tractor and clamber back up and it's all a good laugh.

Though I do remember one event which wasn't quite so funny. My parents have gone away for the weekend, leaving me in the care of Auntie Mary (my mother's other sister who lived close by) on the farm in Boolavounteen. My other cousins Richard and Eamonn are supposed to be keeping an eye on me while Cissy does the myriad jobs needed to keep the place ticking over.

Richard and Eamonn and I are up in the haggard, pulping

turnips for the cattle (we always eat as much as we pulp – they are so sweet and juicy), and on our way back down to the farm for dinner we have to cross a ditch that has an old dry-stone wall running through it. Eamonn goes over first, followed by Richard, and I bring up the rear.

I place my hand on the old wall to get purchase, and, as if in slow motion, I see the whole structure start to come down on top of me. As if it is a living, breathing being, the wall swallows my hand, crushing bones and flesh alike.

The pain is surprising, and it happens so fast I don't even cry out. Instinctively, I pull back, and as I do so, I see blood seeping between the rubble like a bubbling spring. At that, I howl for all I'm worth! The two boys disappear like a shot at the sound, convinced they will be killed for allowing their young charge to come to such harm.

In a flurry of movement, I manage to free myself and run, cradling my injured fingers, to the next yard, which is owned by the Kirwans, Minnie and Eddie, a childless couple who are always very good to me. I barrel into their kitchen and fling myself on the stone floor, declaiming that I have been caught in an avalanche and am probably going to lose my whole arm!

In the manner of country folk who have seen everything and are impressed by nothing, the Kirwans cast a cold eye over me and assure me I will be fine. Minnie calmly produces an old steel milk bucket, fills it with cold well water and plunges my hand into its depths. If my fingers had been sore beforehand, the shock of the icy-cold water is even worse – I am sure I will pass out.

After ten minutes of wailing and repeated submergences, I am brought back to Auntie Mary. My mangled digits are closely examined, and it is decided that Nellie Power, a neighbour who happens to be a nurse, should be sent for. By the time she arrives I am feeling sick from the pain and loss of blood and promptly throw up my breakfast along with quite a bit of raw semi-pulped turnip all over the parlour floor.

The upshot of all this is that, by five that evening, I am in a room in Ardkeen Hospital in Waterford City and Auntie Mary is being asked to sign a form that will give the surgeon permission to remove my finger, which is considered unsavable.

The poor woman is beside herself with worry – in the age before mobile phones, there is no way she can contact my parents to inform them that she has been thoroughly delinquent in her duty. In the end, Mary flatly refuses to sign – how could she take responsibility for such a decision? I come from a family of musicians, she informs the doctors – suppose I decide at some point that I want to play the accordion, like my father?

In a lengthy operation the surgeons rebuild the finger, and by the time Monday rolls around and my parents return, I am perched on the couch in the sitting room in Boolavounteen beside my fractious aunt, my hand strapped up but otherwise none the worse for wear. My mother is as stoic as ever, and after her initial enquiries as to how such a thing came to pass, she shrugs and changes the subject.

My father pets me and insists on overseeing the changing of the dressing (Nellie Power calls nightly to help with the process), but there is no more fuss than that.

Poor Eamonn and Richard give our house a wide berth for weeks after the incident, convinced they'll be flayed for allowing the injury to happen on their watch. I could have told them: flesh and bone heal – in fact, they mend quite quickly.

Injuries to the heart last much longer.

In the summer months the Travelling people come to Boolavounteen. They are called Connors and are from somewhere around Lemybrien, and they set up camp on the roadside just below Cissy's farm. Me and my cousins spend all our spare time with them, sitting on a block by the open fire, listening to their songs and stories. They are always welcome in our house, and if they are on their way back from a fair or a patron, they often stop in to see my mother, who makes them sandwiches and asks about their relatives.

They come every year to fix the buckets and the farming tools, and they are greatly respected by the local people. My friends and I miss them when they leave. It is as if something ancient and tenuous had passed on.

Summer leaves with a breath of honeysuckle and the gentle sigh of the breeze.

The winter is coming. And it is going to be a hard one.

Married on the Radio

The house is frantic.

I'm eleven years old and everywhere I turn there's someone rushing here and running there. I try to find a quiet spot and make my way into the short hallway between the kitchen and the living room – I sometimes go there to sit on the stairs – but there's a young fella I don't even know perched on the bottom step, scribbling something in a notebook. He's dressed in a suit that is far too expensive to belong to one of the Touraneena locals, which means he's from RTÉ. I glare at him, but he doesn't even notice, so I stomp on past and make my way upstairs.

Tisha and Batty are getting married today. I'm excited about it and looking forward to the ceremony and the party afterwards (to be honest, I'm looking forward to the party *much* more), but it was announced last week that the ceremony and some of the reception are going to be broadcast on the national radio by Donncha Ó Dúlaing.

Donncha is a great friend of my father's and is one of the biggest stars on Irish radio and television. His programme *Highways and Byways* is massively popular, and he is famous for doing walks for charity (people can do the walks with him and raise money through sponsorship) – he's done them all over Ireland and in other parts of the world, too.

Donncha knows Daddy through traditional-music circles, and they walked together in the Holy Land. Everyone knows that having the wedding put out live on Radio 1 is really a sign of appreciation for my father, but it's also a reflection of how important a local figure Batty is – it's kind of a coming together of the old and the new: the daughter of the celebrated singer, box-player and set-dancer marrying the up-and-coming rock musician. It's the type of thing *Highways and Byways* often features: the changing face of rural Ireland.

I tiptoe along the landing and glance into Tisha's room. My mammy is in there, helping her do her hair and make-up. The enormous white dress is hanging on the wardrobe door, and I think it looks like something you'd see a princess in a fairy tale wearing. Tisha spies me peeping and flashes me a grin.

She's twelve years older than me, but we're very close, and I'm going to be in the bridal party – a flower girl. She comes out and gives me a quick hug and goes over what I have to do in the church – it's crucial we get everything exactly right because, now that RTÉ is going to be there, the newspapers will be taking photographs and our every move will be under scrutiny. The wedding is the biggest news to hit Touraneena in years.

I promise that I will concentrate hard and won't put a foot wrong.

'You're my favourite youngest sister, you know,' Tisha tells me.

'You've only got one youngest sister!' I laugh.

'That's why you're my favourite!' she says. 'Now you'd better get your dress on, hadn't you?'

I'm still wearing my jeans and sweatshirt.

'OK,' I sigh.

I've always been a bit of a tomboy, and while I appreciate that the dress they've got for me cost a lot of money, I could take it or leave it. I put on the dress, which is blue and actually quite stylish. I've pinched some make-up from Deedee and apply a little to my face. Standing back, I take in my look in the mirror on my bedroom door. I hardly recognise the person I see in the glass. I look quite grown-up and I'm not sure I like it.

I go to the bathroom and, using a facecloth, I scrub off the make-up. Now I feel more like myself.

A big black car takes us to the church. My dad is beaming with pleasure, Mammy looks like one of the cast of *Dallas* and Tisha seems to have stepped right out of a Disney cartoon. Deedee winks at me, and we all line up to have our photographs taken. There seems to be an army of photographers, and I get a pain in my face from all the smiling.

It's all a bit unreal, and I think I'm actually a little bit hypnotised by the lights and the shouting because, before I know it, we're inside the church, with its cavernous space, intense smell of incense and cool air, and the organ is playing, and we're moving through the dappled stained-glass light towards the altar.

I'm at the back of the procession, and I can see around Tisha and Daddy, and there, at the top of the aisle, grinning from ear to ear, is Batty Prendergast. He's wearing a pastel-blue suit over a white shirt and the collar seems too tight – there's a roll of fat spilling over it, and for a second he seems almost grotesque.

We reach the altar rail and I move off to the side, cameras still flashing, and the priest begins to intone the Entrance Antiphon, and I see the microphones with their RTÉ stands and there is Donncha Ó Dúlaing, with a huge pair of headphones on.

My sister is looking at her groom, her eyes wide with love. The photograph of this will appear in the local paper the following week.

I know that things will never be the same again.

Bless This House

After they come back from their honeymoon, Tisha and Batty move to a house he has bought in Tallow, a small town half an hour's drive from Touraneena. The house has three storeys, which seems huge to me.

On the ground floor, Tisha opens a hairdressing salon, and I start helping out there right away – at first I sweep up and make tea, but as time passes and I get more interested and more enthusiastic to learn, she begins to apprentice me and later I get to wash hair and be much more hands-on.

On the second floor are the living room and kitchen, with the bedrooms and bathroom on the top floor.

Because I'm helping out so much, after a while I start to stay there most weekends and on school holidays. No one thinks anything of this, as we are such a close family, and Tisha and I always got on.

And, to my delight, Batty has started to take an interest in me.

Almost everyone sees this as an example of how kind and good-natured my new brother-in-law is. The house in Tallow is very like the Hickey home place, in that it operates an open-door policy and there are always friends, neighbours and family on both sides coming and going. I feel as if the place is just an extension of our house in Touraneena.

The only one who seems a bit reluctant for me to be over there constantly is my dad. I think it's because I'm his baby girl, and he misses having me under his feet so much. But maybe it's something else.

In my eyes, Batty is just like another big brother. In the summer, he and Tisha take me on days out to the beach, where he races me to the water and shows me secluded rock pools and coves where no one else goes. He tells me how good a swimmer I am and observes the muscles in my legs and how flat my tummy is. I blush, but I'm secretly pleased – it's not sexual or a crush, it's that he's a grown-up and, coming from a big family, getting all this one-on-one attention is wonderful. And it's nice to be praised.

We go shopping in Cork and Batty buys me clothes and takes me to a record store and lets me pick out whatever tapes I want. I love Motown stuff – Dionne Warwick is my favourite, and of course Batty knows every single song on the album. We play it in the van all the way home and he sings along, putting on harmonies and beating out the rhythm on the steering wheel.

Because he plays in the band and is out most evenings

at the weekend, friends come over to have dinner early in the evening, and if I'm there, I'm always included in the conversation. It makes me feel part of their social circle rather than a kid who just happens to be around.

Tisha sometimes goes to the houses of elderly clients on a Sunday and they often want her to visit early, before mass, so she goes to bed around ten most Saturdays and I stay up and watch the late film. Sometimes I'll fall asleep in front of the television and wake up as Batty arrives in after his gig.

He is always glad to see me, and, as I make him a cup of tea, he chats about how the night has gone. What I love about these late-night conversations is that he talks to me as if I am an equal. If there was a problem with the sound system or if the drummer missed a cue or if someone requested a song he wasn't sure of, he'll tell me all about it as if I fully understand the trials and tribulations of a pub musician. Sometimes he asks my advice on whether he should add this song to the setlist or stop performing that one. Sometimes he tells me about a new song he's heard that he'd like to learn, and he'll produce a tape he's recorded off the radio. Then, with the volume low, so as not to wake Tisha, we'll sit huddled close together, listening quietly, and he'll point out the musical hook and tell me why it's so good or explain how the harmony line is below the main vocal not than above it.

He seems so smart and so talented and I feel so lucky to have him in the family.

But my luck is about to change.

The Shadows

It's a Friday evening. I am finished school for the week, so as usual I am to stay with Batty and Tisha in Tallow, as I'm helping out in the salon on Saturday. I've packed a small bag with a change of clothes and my hairbrush and some tapes, and Mammy is insisting I eat before leaving, and I'm telling her that I'll have dinner later with Tisha.

The door opens and Batty bustles in, a laugh literally bursting from his barrel chest. He greets my mother warmly, puts a hand on my father's shoulder and tousles my hair. He is wearing jeans so pale they are almost white, and they are so tight they look a little uncomfortable. His T-shirt, which has the Pepsi insignia on it, has ridden up a bit over the dome of his stomach, and his hair has been cut over his ears and is parted down the middle. This evening, he is wearing aviator sunglasses, like Tom Cruise in *Top Gun*.

'Are you ready to go, Steffie?' he asks. 'I've a stop to make along the way, and Tisha wants us back for dinner before I head out to the gig.'

'I told you!' I sigh in a very teenage way to my mother. 'Tisha has dinner for me.'

'Be on your way then,' Mammy says indulgently.

Batty has a sky-blue HiAce van that he uses to bring his sound equipment – speakers and mike stands and guitar cases – to his pub gigs. Usually it is full of gear on a Friday, but oddly it is empty this evening. I hop up beside him.

He is playing 'Walk of Life' by Dire Straits on the stereo in the van as we drive. The *Brothers in Arms* album is very popular just then, and he has been learning some of the songs from it, although he admits to me he doesn't really like Mark Knopfler, the lead singer.

'He looks like he should be working on a building site, not fronting a rock band,' he says sniffily. 'No style at all.'

I always think the English singer and guitarist looks quite nice, but I keep the opinion to myself – I never like to disagree with Batty. He can be quite scary when he gets cross.

Near Ballyduff is a beauty spot called Lismore Towers. It is a secluded wooded walkway leading to a ruined castle and a couple of waterfalls. It's not on our usual route to

Tallow, but Batty had said he needed to make a stop, so at first I don't think anything of it. There aren't any houses around here, but maybe he's meeting someone.

I sit back and listen to the music. Batty, who usually chats non-stop, has become uncharacteristically quiet.

It is October, and it is already dark. A light rain is drizzling, and the area doesn't seem very inviting. As the van winds along the narrow pathway between the trees, I wonder who on earth my brother-in-law could possibly be meeting all the way out here.

We reach a clearing and he pulls the van over so it is partially hidden by an outcropping branch and switches off the engine.

'Come on,' he says.

'Where to?' I ask, genuinely puzzled.

'Let's get in the back.'

I'm really confused now. 'Why?'

He doesn't look at me, just opens the driver's side door and hops down, sliding open the panel and waiting for me to follow.

'I said: *come on!*'

I shrug and do as I'm told. Maybe he needs me to help him move something. I don't see what it could be, but Batty is always full of surprises.

There is carpet on the floor of the van, and I notice he has laid a sleeping bag on top of it. I climb in and pull my knees up to my chest. He gets in beside me and closes the door.

'What's going on, Batty?'

He doesn't say anything, but I don't like the way he's looking at me. He reaches out his hand and touches my face, but then he's not touching my face any more, he's touching places no one has touched before. I try to move away but within two shuffles my back is against the side of the van and there's nowhere else to go. And then it starts and I can't stop it and inside my head I'm screaming: *No! No! No!* but no sound is coming and there's nothing I can do.

I am twelve years old.

I have never had a boyfriend and I have never been kissed and the only time anyone other than my parents or siblings have put their hands on me, which was always with unconditional, pure familial love, has been friends in rough-and-tumble play or for a friendly hug. In the Ireland of the 1980s sex is never discussed, and when a love scene comes on the television in the Hickey household, the channel is changed quick smart.

What is happening to me now is disorienting and foul.

I am confused and frightened and I feel nauseous. He seems huge above me, and he is trying to take my clothes off, and I struggle weakly and then just freeze. Instinctively, I close my eyes and some part of my brain tells me that it will be over, sooner or later, and if I can just endure it, I will be all right.

I don't know how I knew that – maybe it is a cellular memory women have.

Now he is taking his clothes off. He is pale and flabby and he is wearing what I now know to be thong underpants and I have never seen underwear like that before and they add an even more bizarre twist to what seems to be a nightmare. He is hard against me and his voice is hoarse and his mouth is all over me and then he tells me to do something to him and I balk because what he asks seems so sick and so wrong and he is married to my sister, to Tisha. He forces my head down and I can't breathe, but he doesn't seem to care. He is making moaning sounds and I feel a part of me disconnect and drift away.

I thought he was like a brother.

I thought I could trust him.

Outside, the shadows grow longer.

CENTRAL CRIMINAL COURT, DUBLIN

AUGUST 2018

During the Lunch Break

When the judge states that the cases will not be heard separately, that Batty's bid to alleviate the severity of his sentence has failed, I break down in a flood of tears. It feels like, for the first time, someone in a position of authority has acknowledged how serious what happened to me and Deedee was.

I double over on the bench and sob.

Time stalls, and then Michael Murphy, one of the barristers for the DPP, Director of Public Prosecutions, is beside us and he's telling us that court won't resume for at least an hour. I don't want to go back up to the green room – I need space and air and a change of scenery. Clare, my court liaison, tells me there is a nice little restaurant just

43

across the road from the Four Courts; a lot of the legal staff go there.

I'm not really interested in eating, but I agree to go and the whole family, along with Michael and the other barrister for the DPP, Noel Whelan, troop over. I'm handed a menu, but all the items seem to swim together and I mutter that I'll just have a bowl of soup. Someone puts a cup of tea in my hands and I sip that. The soup arrives, but I couldn't even tell you what kind it is – I go through the motions of spooning some into my mouth, but it has no flavour and I set it aside.

My phone rings. I make my excuses and head for the door, but I'm still in shock and I can't make sense of the phone's handset, although I've been using it for more than a year. I have stopped walking and am trying to answer the call when I hear my eldest brother, Richard, call to me to come back. I turn to look at him in annoyance, about to tell him that I have to answer the phone, when I hear footsteps approaching, and snapping my head forward, I see that Batty has just walked into the restaurant with one of his legal team, a woman whose name I don't know.

For the first time since all of this started, we are eye to eye.

It feels odd to have him so physically close to me again. I can smell his aftershave and the product he is using in his hair. I actually hear the rustle as his hand opens and closes on that ridiculous plastic bag. The restaurant is full and has been busy since we arrived, waiting staff bustling in and out of the kitchen with orders, and there is a buzz of conversation, but at this moment it is just him and me.

I should be scared. I should be angry.

I feel nothing.

Something registers in his eyes – I don't know what it is, perhaps the calculating survival instinct of a cornered animal – and without a word, he and the woman turn on their heel and are gone. The world snaps back into focus, and Richard is at my side, telling me it's OK and leading me back to the table.

But I'm all right.

We came face to face, and this time, he backed down.

Maybe I'm on a winning streak.

So You Believe Me?

We get back to court, and I begin to fixate on negative things again. I know I shouldn't, but the thoughts come unbidden.

The first day in court, when the case was adjourned, was the worst of them all.

There was the tense wait for the judge to come in from his chambers – I passed the time looking around the room again, taking it all in.

I remember noticing that Batty's legal team – his two barristers – were both female.

I wondered what it must be like to be a female lawyer and to cross-examine another woman about her experience of being raped or sexually abused. To try to pick holes in her story. It occurred to me that these women were chosen by their firm because it casts Batty in a more favourable light – *sure he can't be too bad, look, his team are all women.*

I realised, then, that the case was making me cynical and I don't like that in myself. But I couldn't help these thoughts going through my head. I looked at the female barristers again and reminded myself that this was just their job, and that someone had to do it. It's the way the legal system works. But what a terrifying system to be caught up in.

The judge came in that first day and Batty was asked to rise. The charges were read, and there were thirteen counts of sexual assault and two of rape, regarding my case alone. I sat there, stunned by the fact that this was all relating to me, and I leaned over and asked my liaison, Clare, 'Why are they still calling my name?'

I had thought there were five counts in all.

'Your lawyers have gone through your statement and broken your story down,' she told me. 'I know it seems an awful lot, but this is better, I promise. It'll be much harder for him to argue against. There's a lot of detail his team will have to get to grips with.'

I nodded and felt the tears coming. Suddenly, despite all my efforts, I could feel myself shrinking and in a heartbeat I was that twelve-year-old girl all over again, sitting naked, cold and alone, being judged by all these educated, highfalutin people. Could all this stuff have happened to me? I'd spent so much time blocking it out, not allowing myself to think about it, that having it all laid out was almost overwhelming.

I remember my whole body had started to shake, and I couldn't stop it. The trembles lasted for about twenty minutes. Angelo, my partner, spotted that I was in trouble right away and without a word put his hand gently on my leg to stop it thudding off the floor. Clare quietly whispered to me that it would be OK and held down my other leg, which was jigging up and down of its own accord, too. I apologised and explained I couldn't control it.

I knew I was going into shock, and there was nothing I could do but ride it out.

As each charge was read, Batty was asked what his plea was: guilty or not guilty.

For each one, he calmly intoned the words: 'Not guilty.'

I wanted to scream every time he said it because it felt like he was really saying: *she's the guilty one!*

This is what is going through my head when we come back into the court for the afternoon, after I have confronted him in the restaurant. My dark thoughts are interrupted by a kerfuffle at the top of the room between Michael Murphy, the barrister, and one of the defence team. There is a heated discussion of some kind that I can't hear, and Michael looks down at me suddenly. I can't read his expression – there's something extreme in it, but I don't know what it is. It could be anger or frustration or anxiety – I'm just not certain. Then they all bustle out of one of the doors at the top.

I don't know what to make of this – I think something must have gone badly wrong and I'm panicked. What if they've decided it's all been a big mistake and they're dropping the charges and this has all been for nothing? I feel the room spinning, and even though everyone is telling me it's going to be fine, I can't hear it. Nothing is going in.

The whole room falls silent.

Silence is a strange thing. Usually, it is all the little noises you can hear when all the big sounds are gone. Even then, you'll have people fiddling with their phones or chatting quietly, there'll be the creaking of a chair as someone shifts their weight, the puffing, blowing exhalation that comes from secretive vaping, the distant caw of a rook outside the window.

In the courtroom there is none of that. Everyone sits looking dead forward. Not a single phone is produced, no one talks, there is utter, complete, total silence – you could literally hear a pin drop. It is deeply unsettling and unfathomably eerie. Because Deedee and I have decided to waive our anonymity, the media are present in court, but even they have become muted, the usual clatter of keyboards and hushed exchanges ceasing as we await whatever is going to happen next.

I chance a look at Batty, but as usual he just sits there, cradling his plastic bag, lost in his own world. I wonder if he is singing a song in his head: something by Johnny Cash maybe. How does he stay so calm? Is he even human at all?

I turn my focus inward.

No matter what the next hour brings, I tell myself, you have achieved something. You are here, in one of the highest courts in the land. You have stood up and made people listen. You have gotten control of your own narrative and spoken your truth.

If nothing else comes from all this, I know I can cling to that. The thought gives me strength. I reach down inside and find my younger self and tell her: *I've got you. No matter what, this is all for you. Your suffering has not gone unnoticed.*

Twenty minutes pass. I'm barely aware, because I have gone inside myself so deeply, but Deedee is called outside by one of the gardaí. Ten more minutes go by, and I'm still in the depths of my being with my teenage self. Someone taps me on the shoulder, and it is the same garda.

'Can you come outside for a moment, Stephanie?'

I grab Angelo. 'Can you come with me?' I ask, convinced something has gone terribly wrong.

Outside the big double doors of the courtroom, Deedee and my brother Richard are huddled together, and both are crying. He hugs me. I'm too terrified to say anything or ask what is going on.

I'm led into a small meeting room – it contains a round table, four chairs and nothing else. Michael Murphy and Noel Whelan are both sitting facing the door.

'Stephanie, we've had a breakthrough,' Michael says in his gentle, steady way.

I blink and motion with my head for him to continue.

'Stephanie, he's going to plead guilty.'

I hear the words but they don't mean anything at first.

'I don't understand,' I stammer. 'Do you mean that it's over?'

'Well, not quite, there'll have to be a sentencing of course, but in theory, yes. You've won.'

I start crying again. I seem to be doing little else today.

'So you believe me?' I ask him through my tears.

He laughs and takes my hands.

'I never *didn't* believe you!' he says.

And I don't remember much more after that.

Holding My Head Up High

I'm told it's over, but I can't believe it. I keep expecting someone to tell me there has been a mistake, or that some paperwork has gone missing, and that we're back at square one or worse.

As we walk out of the broom-cupboard-sized room where the barristers have just informed us Batty is pleading guilty, I ask Angelo where David Mansfield, the garda from Ballymacarbery is – he's the person I made my statement to three years ago, and he promised me he would be there for the duration of the trial.

How could he have left me now, right at the end?

Angelo looks at me in surprise. 'Stephanie, he was sitting beside Noel Whelan. He's right behind us.'

I turn and there he is. I know I'm not functioning properly at all – he was sitting in front of me and I literally did not see him.

We are brought back into the main courtroom. Tears are pouring down my face in twin rivers and I make no effort to stop them. Moments later (or it could be hours, I don't know any more) the judge, Justice Creedon, comes in, and we are told to rise. The charges are read all over again so Batty can offer his new plea.

I hang my head, unable to believe I have to endure this litany for a third time. Clare whispers in my ear, 'Stephanie, try and keep your head up. Look him in the eye.'

I don't know if I can. Beside me and Angelo on the bench are my kids: they are all adults and want to be here to support me, and I am grateful for that, but how can they not think less of me when they hear all the things I allowed to happen? Every time this shopping list of debasement is recounted, it feels as if I am being called out as a weak, promiscuous slattern. I am deeply ashamed.

'Hold your head high!' Clare whispers again. 'Every time he says "guilty", look right at him and let him know you are hearing it and that it means that after all these years, you've won. You'll never have this moment again – take what good you can from it.'

I would love to say that I immediately pull myself upright and stand tall and strong, but that would be a lie.

For the first couple of minutes I keep my eyes lowered, but as each count is read and my abuser responds with *guilty* something starts to build in me, and gradually my head comes up and I gaze at him.

'Good for you!' Clare says, squeezing my hand.

She's right. I definitely get *some* closure from watching him. But he is still so damned composed. It is as if he has simply changed his mind and it cost him nothing to do it – either way would have been fine. He does not appear stressed or upset or remotely concerned about what is going on.

Batty stands there, his awful plastic bag held tightly in his fists, and airily responds to each description of the foul deeds that brought us all to this place. From the first charge to the fifteenth, his voice remains calm, resonant and strong. There are no tears drying on his cheeks as there are on mine, no tremble to his stance and no shame or sadness marring his facial expression.

I suddenly understand that what I am seeing is Batty the showman – the performer. This is just another gig for him, and the people crushed into the seats in the Central Criminal Court are another pub audience. He's had the press at his beck and call before, at his wedding to Tisha and at some of his famous golf tournaments. He's used to the adulation and the infamy.

He's been training for this moment all his life.

They finish the charges associated with me and go on to those for Deedee. The whole thing takes more than an hour, and throughout my brother-in-law is unruffled. When the last count is read, Batty is led to the top of the court and signs a document confirming that he has pled guilty to all charges brought against him. I watch his stride and marvel at how confident and steady he seems. He executes his signature with a flourish, as if he is signing an autograph.

Everyone sits back down, and now I'm excited and anxious. This is the bit I've really been waiting for: the sentencing. I've served over thirty years of pain and anguish for what my brother-in-law did to me. Now I get to see what kind of punishment he will receive.

Justice Creedon is busily writing something on a legal pad in front of her. We all wait, tense and on edge. Finally she looks up. 'As I have only just been handed this brief,' she says, choosing each word carefully, 'I do not feel prepared to hand down sentence yet. I need some time to read back over all the documentation and to give due consideration to the victim impact statements.'

At this moment, one of Batty's barristers shoots up from her seat. 'Judge, my client requests that some character references be entered into the record on his behalf also. He has a long history of public service in his locality, and he believes such community-minded conduct should not be disregarded.'

Justice Creedon looks down at Batty without expression. 'I think I'd like to hear the victim impact statements first,' she says sternly.

Michael Murphy stands and nods in my direction.

For the first time in the whole process, I am going to tell my story in my own words. I'm going to tell Bartholomew Prendergast just what I think of him.

I'm about to give evidence in court.

WEST WATERFORD

THE 1980s

A Lesson That I Never Knew

Batty Prendergast is leaning against the sink in the house in Tallow. His arms are folded across his chest and he is telling me about a golf tournament he just won. All the important people from west Waterford were playing: politicians, big businessmen, his bosses in the council – Batty went up against them all and emerged victorious.

My brother-in-law never drank and he never smoked, but he tells me that he went along to the bar in the clubhouse after the tournament and allowed them to buy him 7-Up all evening. He reckoned he was entitled to it after playing so well.

I notice he is very pleased with himself this afternoon. And that makes me nervous.

From a drawer at his hip he produces a cardboard envelope full of photographs and passes them to me so I can share in his victory. Batty owns a top-of-the-line Canon camera and takes it everywhere with him. The house is full of all the latest gadgets and technology, and he can take apart any item and put it back together again. He's a lot of things, is Batty Prendergast, but stupid isn't one of them.

I try to focus on the images before me, but it's difficult.

My brother-in-law is dressed in his usual skin-tight, high-waisted jeans and his erection is obscenely visible through the material. Tisha is downstairs in the salon. She could come upstairs at any moment. But I know Batty doesn't care. I think he enjoys the risk, the chance we might get caught.

I make an excuse and go upstairs to the room Tisha has told me to think of as my own. There are only three rooms on the third floor – mine; Tisha and Batty's; and off that a kind of box-room that currently has a small single bed and a few storage containers with electrical gear.

I close the door and put my Dionne Warwick tape into my Walkman. There's a song called 'Heartbreaker' on it that I really love. I pull myself into a foetal position on the bed, scrunch closed my eyes and sing along with Dionne. Her voice is so soothing, and the music seems to ease my stress away.

The door to my room is shoved open. I don't need to look up – I know it's him. I hear his voice over the beauty of the music, and it sounds so coarse and ugly.

'Come on.'

There's no point in fighting or employing delaying tactics – I know by now that it's better to get it done. I'll be safe afterwards, for a while at least. I switch off the music and put the Walkman aside. Batty is waiting for me on the landing. He is completely naked and fully erect. He leads me into his and Tisha's room and through to the box-room beyond. I see he has fitted a full-length mirror to the door.

'Do it here. So I can watch you.'

I get on my knees.

He's moaning and making strange noises. I chance a look at our reflection and see he's someplace else, wrapped up in his own pleasure. At his knees is a terrified, hollow-eyed child. I realise she is me.

After what seems an age, he picks me up and flings me on the bed. He takes my clothes off roughly, gets on top of me and puts it inside me. It hurts so badly I think I'm going to die. I start to cry out and he puts his hand over my mouth and keeps going until he's finished.

'It'll get better,' he says when he climbs off me. 'You'll see. Making love always hurts a bit at first.'

That is how I lost my virginity: with a coarse hand pressed over my mouth, wracked with agony in a small room in my sister's house. Batty called it 'making love'.

I found out years later that the proper name for it is rape.

Out of Control

I'm thirteen years old and I'm being regularly abused by my brother-in-law, my sister's husband. He is loved by my family and respected and adored by my friends and neighbours. I am a regular visitor to his and Tisha's house (Batty's arrival at the old schoolhouse on a Friday evening to bring me to Tallow is now a weekly ritual).

And I would give anything to never go to that house again.

The problem is that I don't have a clue how to even broach the subject with my parents. Looking back, I understand that I didn't have the vocabulary – I had no words for some of the things he made me do.

I reasoned that I could tell my mother I didn't like Batty

any more, but she would immediately want to know why and that would mean trying to explain, and Tisha would be called in, and I really did not want to face her and tell her what he had done ... what *I* had done.

That left me the option of lying, of making something up, but I couldn't think of anything that would get me out of the Friday-evening trips but that wouldn't lead to even more questions – I would have to tell lies to back up the lies I had already told, and I'm no good at keeping that kind of subterfuge going. I forget what I've said and it all comes tumbling down. I realised with dawning horror that I was trapped.

I had no choice but to keep going to Tallow and to just hope the molestation would stop, that he would lose interest.

Of course, he didn't. It just got worse.

After each instance of abuse took place, Batty would behave as if it had never happened. He would laugh and joke and treat me in the same thoughtful and seemingly kind manner he did before it started. In his home, I rarely had to make myself a drink or do any chores outside of the salon because Batty would fuss over me and treat me like a princess. Even when it was just me and him on our own, the sexual aspect of our relationship was simply not mentioned or referred to. It was as if a figurative wall had been built around it – it was something that existed only when Batty decided he wanted his pleasure, but other than that it was not to be spoken of.

But gradually, his appetites began to run out of control, and it was like I wasn't safe anywhere.

The trips to the beach that I used to look forward to became excuses for a kind of sex tourism. Tisha would set up the picnic or relax with her book, and Batty would announce that he was going to teach me to swim. Taking me by the hand, I would be brought down to the water – despite being a strong swimmer, I have a fear of the ocean to this day and won't go beyond my knees. The only place I will swim is in an indoor pool where I am surrounded by people.

Batty would lead me out into the deeper water, so it came up to our chests, and he would put my hand down his trunks and have me masturbate him. Sometimes he would make me go under the water and take him in my mouth.

Other times, he would lead me to those secluded spots he knew across the rocks, and he would have intercourse with me. The only plus to all of this was that once he was finished he would stop annoying me and we could get on with the day. I'm ashamed to say that, but it's the truth.

The beach was called Whiting Bay – you had to traverse a boreen to get to it (Batty never went to busy beaches) – and I have never been back there since. I feel a tremble of revulsion even driving past the signpost for it, near Ardmore.

Things are even worse back in Tallow.

Batty has started to walk around the house naked –

Tisha will be downstairs in the salon, and it does not seem to worry him that she might arrive upstairs at any moment. In fact, I think he enjoys the frisson of danger.

He seems to be constantly taking showers and changing clothes, and he will always find an excuse to call down for me to bring him up something. Even when I'm in the salon I'm not safe, as Batty has installed intercoms so he can call down and have me sent up to him.

I am literally forced to jump every time he wants some attention.

Upstairs I go, treading each step slowly, knowing what is waiting for me when I get up to the third floor. On these afternoons, he can take his time, as there is no way Tisha will leave her customers.

Batty starts to want me to go shopping with him or to accompany him on trips to pick up instruments or equipment. There are three seats in the front of his van, and he makes me sit in the middle one, right beside him. As soon as we hit a long stretch of road, he makes me open his trousers and give him a blow job as he drives.

This is one of his favourite things. I can still feel his hand on the back of my head, controlling the pressure. It doesn't matter how much I retch and choke, he only seems to like it more.

I beg him not to make me do it, but his response is always the same: *No one will see you, just lie down and open wide!* It's as if the pain and the nausea I experience are just not a factor – he can only see things from his own point of view.

Through all of this horror, I hear the sounds of him moaning in pleasure, whispering sounds of happiness and ecstasy, and I am appalled that anyone could find such joy in these acts of sickness.

And even though I am just thirteen, and even though he still calls what he forces me to do 'making love', I know he has no feelings for me.

He does not fancy me or care about me. I am just a vessel for his twisted desires.

What eats away at me is why he chose me. What is it in me that made him pluck me out of all the girls he is in regular contact with?

The belief that I did something to bring this torment on myself still hasn't really gone away. Maybe one day it will, but it is his lasting gift to me, a stain upon myself.

I hate him for it.

Mary

Mary is my friend – that is not her real name, but it is what I am going to call her here. She chose not to be named, and I will respect that wish.

I met her through some friends shortly after my sister came to Tallow, and we quickly became really close. Hanging out with her gives me an excuse not to spend every waking moment in the house when I come to stay with my sister – when Batty seems unhappy with my going out with my new pal, Tisha hushes him, saying that it's good for me to have some friends of my own age. I can see this annoys my brother-in-law, but he can't seem to come up with a good reason to keep me at home.

Mary is a member of a local sports club, and she urges me to join too. Poking around the house, I spy a very fancy-looking hurley, all wrapped in colourful tape with a beautiful fluorescent flannel hand grip, and jars of sliotars high up on a shelf in the box-room, the place Batty takes me for sex. I know that Batty plays hurling occasionally, although I don't think he's very good at it. Being the type of man he is, he has the most expensive new-fangled-looking equipment on the market. This hurley looks like it has never even been used so I ask Tisha if Mary and I can use it. She can't think of a reason not to give it to me, so I have a beautiful new hurley.

I know Batty is furious about this, but there isn't much he can say about it either, so I'm doubly happy.

My weekends seem a little brighter with Mary in them, and when we're able to, we both head into town with my meagre wages and buy chips and hang out. Mary likes the same kind of music and is funny and clever and it is just great to have a friend.

One evening we are sitting on the wall outside her house, and we are talking about boys we think we might like when Mary mentions Batty.

'What do you think of him?' she asks me

The conversation immediately goes silent. Neither of us is looking at the other.

'I don't like him,' I say at last.

'Why not?'

I fiddle with the cuff of my jacket. 'I can't tell you,' I say, my voice little more than a whisper.

I can feel tears lurking behind my eyes, and I don't want my new friend to see me crying. She seems to notice I'm on the verge of breaking down and puts her arm around me.

'You can tell me anything, you know,' she says, and before I can stop myself, the words are out.

'Batty does things to me.'

I am shocked at myself, but it's too late. I can't unsay it.

Mary sighs and rubs her eyes. I see, to my complete surprise, that she is crying now, too. 'You mean *sex* things,' she says.

'Yes,' I croak.

'He does things to me, too,' she says, and I feel the world spinning and for a moment I think I might faint.

I'm not alone. It's not just me. The knowledge gives me a strength that seems almost superhuman. We look at each other, eyes liquid and wide, and without even saying the words, we know what we have to do.

We have to tell.

Batty's Women

Batty is on stage with his band. We're at a gig in Waterford City: me, Tisha and an old schoolfriend of hers, Liam, who often joins us when we go to see Stardust play.

To be clear, I don't want to be here, but every time I try to make an excuse not to come, Tisha launches an interrogation, and I end up going anyway. It's easier just to grit my teeth and put up with it.

The band are playing Bryan Adams' 'Summer of '69'. The room is crowded and the ceiling is low and the sound from the speakers is a bit overdriven and harsh, but no one seems to mind. Batty and his sidemen are crushed on the tiny stage at the end of the bar, and people are clustered in front of them in a tight pack.

At the front of the stage is a woman who has probably had a little bit too much to drink. In between songs she loudly shouts up her appreciation, not just of the music, but of Batty himself. She seems to know him – he hasn't introduced the band yet (he usually doesn't do that until the end of the night), but she knows his name and keeps on saying things like: 'Come on now, Batty, give us a smoochy one!' or 'Turn up that ould guitar, Batty – you're the one we want to hear!'

For his part, Batty winks and grins at her, never failing to comment back: 'I'll give you a smooch all right, Kathy!' and 'You'll be hearin' plenty from me later on, don't worry!'

What amazes me is that he says these things right into the microphone – if Tisha can hear him, she doesn't let on for a second. She chats away to Liam, who is a sweet-natured, gentle kind of a man (the polar opposite of Batty), and she seems to be having a grand old time.

The band take a break halfway through the set, and I notice Batty slipping out the back, where there is an old beer garden (it's a wet night, so it will be deserted). A few moments later, Kathy, his loud admirer, heads out after him.

I'm tempted to follow, but to be frank, I don't want to see what is going on out there. I don't need to.

Even before they got married, Batty and Tisha split up several times because Batty had been caught in a clinch with another woman. My family thought that was the end of it, that the relationship was over, but within a week they were reunited. Apparently, he made all kinds of promises that he would behave and not stray again, but shortly after the wedding there was another blow-up when a friend of Tisha's told her she'd seen Batty getting physical with a woman after a gig in Dungarvan.

They worked through it, but the truth is here for all to see: Bartholomew Prendergast is a womaniser – it is a passion for him, a sport, just like golf or squash. He is what the younger people call a 'player'.

Batty enjoys the chase, the flirting, the teasing glances and the double entendres. He is never in any doubt that he is completely irresistible to any female he comes in contact with, regardless of their age, and he is supremely confident in his ability to charm.

The band is the perfect vehicle for this hobby: it's well known that many women will look at a man with a guitar with a desire they would never feel if they saw him without it, and Batty knows this all too well. As far as he is concerned, he is Elvis Presley, Mick Jagger and Tom Jones all wrapped up in one blond package.

What boggles my mind is where he finds the time or the energy. Barely a day goes by when he doesn't have some kind of sexual contact with me, and I know he's interfering with Mary, too. I assume he's being intimate with Tisha, and then there's all these women as well ... Batty eats a lot of steak dinners, but I figure he has to be taking vitamin supplements and consuming a lot of energy drinks too to keep this kind of behaviour up.

It also occurs to me that the kind of hunger Batty seems to have for sex isn't normal. I've grown up around men: my father, my brothers, my cousins and neighbours. They don't behave like this. What I see when I look at my brother-in-law is a man out of control. His urges are in the driving seat, and he's just a passenger.

The problem is, he's on a collision course, and he's taking a lot of us down with him.

The Chasm Opens

Mary and I are walking through Tallow. It is late evening and dusk is coming down. I know there is something on her mind because she is usually so chatty, but tonight she walks with her head lowered and a furrowed brow. We pause at a shop window. It is full of pretty dresses and high-heeled, feminine shoes – items we find fascinating and horrifying in equal measure.

My friend and I are dressed in jumpers, jeans and runners – it's the disguise we wear to hide the fact that our bodies are becoming more curvaceous and womanly. Most girls our age are looking for excuses to maximise the contours nature is bestowing upon them, but not us. Batty has ensured that Mary and I are ashamed of our growing maturity.

He is the only man to have ever touched us sexually – if any boys our own age express even the remotest interest, we run as fast as we can in the opposite direction. I cannot imagine ever being comfortable with physical closeness. The thought of it sickens and terrifies me.

Beside me, Mary heaves a heavy sigh, and I notice she is crying.

'Are you going to tell me what's wrong with you?' I ask as gently as I can.

'Promise you won't get annoyed?'

A part of me (maybe a selfish part) wonders how I can answer that question without first knowing what she is going to say, but I decide to ignore that knee-jerk response and simply tell her that I will remain calm.

'I told my mam about Batty,' she says, the words coming out in a rapid surge, as if she is afraid she won't be able to finish unless she hurries.

It is as if a bucket of freezing-cold water has been dumped on top of me. I know we discussed telling, but it was in a very broad way and was really more an expression that we knew we *should* rather than a plan to actually *do* it.

'What did she say?' I ask, trying to keep the tremble out of my voice.

'She didn't say an awful lot,' Mary responds.

That stumps me for a moment. 'Come on, Mary, she must have said something!'

'She says she's going to call your mam to talk about it.'

And now I want the ground to open up and swallow me.

'So that's it then,' I hear myself say. 'It's all going to come out.'

And we stand for what seems like forever, staring in that shop window, but not really seeing anything.

The Gathering

Mary and I, along with Deedee and her boyfriend Ciaran (who had the bad luck to call in for a visit), are in the living room above the hairdressing salon in Tallow.

In the kitchen are my parents, Mary's mother, Batty and Tisha.

There is a lot of shouting going on. I can particularly hear Mary's mother, who is really angry, but Tisha's voice is very much in evidence, too. Every now and again my mother can be heard (Mammy doesn't shout, but then she doesn't need to – when she talks everyone listens). I strain to hear my father, but if he does speak it is so quiet I can't make it out. But that's Daddy – I know he must be hating all this anger and confrontation.

While I think I know what the purpose of the noisy gathering is, I'm not completely certain. Mary has been very tight-lipped about exactly what she told her mother, so I don't know whether or not my own experiences at the hands of Batty are even being discussed. It's also not clear to me how much detail Mary went into when she told her mother about what happened (I know it is almost identical to my own abuse, but when I ask her what she said, she claims she told her mother Batty 'went at her' and that she didn't like it). Which could be interpreted any number of ways.

Deedee and Ciaran are bewildered and we all sit in silence, wondering what the outcome of the disturbance is going to be.

The arguing back and forth goes on for about an hour. From our vantage point in the living room we can identify who is shouting, but the words are too muffled to be sure what is being said. Finally the door slams open, and Mary's mother emerges, red-faced and in a foul temper.

'We're leaving!' she says and without a word Mary gets up and follows.

Mary's parents have known Tisha and Batty for years, so she has good reason to see this as a terrible betrayal. My parents follow, my father's head bowed, my mother as upright and stern as always.

'You're coming home with us,' my mother says to me. 'Deedee, you should leave too. That pair have some talking to do.'

Deedee throws me a glance, and we all troop downstairs. She came in Ciaran's car, which means I make the journey back to Touraneena sitting silently in the back seat of our Ford as my parents ignore one another in the front.

What happened in that kitchen in Tallow in the late 1980s has never been shared with me. To this day I don't know what was discussed.

And I never asked.

Somehow I felt I had contributed to the grim anger that emanated from everyone who had been there that day, and I just wanted to pretend it was all a dream and would disappear with the morning sun.

I was getting good at doing that.

The Prodigal Son Returns

My parents and I arrive home after the angry meeting in Tallow. My mother storms into the sanctuary of her kitchen and Daddy takes up his seat in the living room. Mammy begins the meditative process of baking some bread (she works off a lot of anger with aggressive kneading) and Daddy pulls out the accordion and starts to play a slow air.

I know this means they both want to be left alone, so I go to my room and stick on some music, my way of soothing life's stresses. Before too long I feel myself start to drift into a doze, but I am roused by the sound of the front door slamming and footsteps clattering up the hallway below.

No one is due to arrive, and I wonder if this is more fallout from Mary's revelations, so I shake myself awake and head downstairs to see what is going on. I step gingerly into the living room to find Tisha, clearly very upset, being comforted by my father. Mammy is perched on the edge of the couch, her face set in an expression of grim tolerance as Daddy strokes Tisha's hair while she sobs.

'Put the kettle on, Stephanie,' Mammy says finally. 'I think we could all do with a cup of tea.'

I understand in a wave of anxiety that Mary has not shared that I was one of Batty's extra-marital diversions.

Tisha stays with us for four days. It is like old times. My big sister and I go for walks on the mountain. We do one another's hair and sit up late watching stupid films and eating sweets. We go shopping together in Dungarvan and we cook a special dinner and invite the whole family (all except Batty). It is a lovely, carefree time and I am grateful for it.

I really believe all the bad stuff is over. At night, before I go to sleep, I whisper a silent prayer of thanks to Mary for doing what I wasn't brave enough to do: for telling what Batty was doing and putting a stop to it.

I wake up on Friday morning and go down for breakfast, full of that sense of happiness and contentment. Singing a Dionne Warwick song merrily to myself, I skip into the kitchen and am stopped dead in my tracks.

Batty is standing at the cooker, his stone-washed jeans stretched tight across his fleshy arse, love handles spilling over his thick leather belt. Mammy is sitting on one side of the table, Tisha the other. They have plates laden with sausages, rashers and eggs in front of them, and a pot of tea, freshly brewed, sits in pride of place on its wicker mat.

'Hello, Stephanie,' Batty says, turning to smirk at me. 'Will I throw on some rashers for you?'

I mumble a response, my head reeling.

'Batty came over today to sort things out,' Tisha says, smiling for all she's worth.

'Your father has rung Father Crowley, over in Clonmel,' Mammy says. 'He's going to have a talk to the pair of them. Help them deal with their marital issues.'

'Lots of couples have problems, don't they, Mammy?' Tisha says, popping a corner of toast into her mouth.

'Every marriage has its ups and downs,' my mother agrees.

I want to be sick. Father Brendan Crowley is a long-time friend of our family's. In rural Ireland in the late 1980s, the parish priest is the person everyone goes to when they have problems: if you lose a baby, you go to the priest; if you are having sexual problems, you go to the priest; if your husband is having sexual relations with underage girls (it seems), you go to the priest.

As I sit down beside my mother and Batty plonks a plate of food in front of me, I pray that Father Crowley can work some kind of magic.

Because as Batty leans against the counter to watch us all eat, he winks at me.

And I know that the hunger he is feeling that morning cannot be satiated by a full Irish.

The Cure

Two weeks pass.

Deedee and I are sitting up late one night after everyone else has gone to bed. She has been hanging around the house a lot lately, and I notice there seems to be a distance between her and Ciaran. I don't know what it is, but I trust my sister will share whatever is bothering her in her own time.

'You know Batty has been going to meetings in Clonmel,' she says to me over a steaming mug of tea.

'I know. Father Crowley is helping him with his "marital" problems,' I say, unable to keep the scorn from my voice.

'I overheard Mammy talking about it,' Deedee says. 'I don't think he's seeing Father Crowley.'

'One of the other priests, then?'

'I was outside the kitchen door, and I heard Mammy ask Daddy how Batty was getting on with the psychiatrist,' Deedee says.

I gasp at that. Psychiatrists are, in my understanding, only called upon when someone is severely ill. In rural Ireland, the idea of going to see a mental health professional to deal with stress or anxiety is a foreign concept. Maybe, I think to myself, Batty's appetites *are* being taken seriously.

'What did Daddy say?'

'He said he didn't know, that Father Crowley was going to call a friend of his who is a head doctor, and after that it is none of our business.'

I drink some of my tea. 'Can a psychiatrist cure a person of ... well, of what's wrong with Batty?'

Deedee gives me a funny look. 'What do you think is wrong with Batty?' she asks.

I splutter, not sure what to say. 'I don't know.' I desperately try to find the right words. 'Not being a good husband, I suppose.'

Deedee seems to sag when I say this. 'For Tisha's sake, I hope he can,' she says. 'Maybe for all our sakes.'

And then she goes to bed.

I sit up long into the night, wondering what that last statement might mean.

Back to Normal

Another week passes, and as Friday rolls around, the phone rings. It is Tisha. She wants to know if I will come down to Tallow to help her in the salon over the weekend. I come up with half a dozen excuses on the spot but can't bring myself to use any of them.

Father Crowley has gotten Batty help, hasn't he? I tell myself. Surely, after all the fuss that has been caused, he won't bother me any more.

Five thirty comes far too soon, and, just like before, the door bursts open and in strides Batty. As always, he fusses over my mother and tells her how wonderful a woman she is and how he feels blessed to be a member of our family.

I wait for her to ask him how the 'treatment' is going, but

she never refers to it. After half an hour of small talk, Batty stands up. 'We'd best be getting on the road,' he calls to me. 'Tisha has some steaks bought for dinner, and I want to get home to make the spud chips. I can't be doin' with frozen ones.'

My mother tells him what a wise man he is to take a stand against mass-produced frozen foods, and together we go out to the van. I get in the front but make a point of sitting over right against the door. Batty seems not to notice, and we begin the journey to Tallow.

I know I'm in trouble when he reaches over and pulls me by the arm so I'm sitting crushed up beside him. 'Shall I make a wee stop along the way, Stephanie?' he asks me, his voice hoarse with excitement.

I want to say no but I just freeze. I can't find my voice. He presses my hand into his groin. It is rock hard and has a pulse of its own.

'How about Lismore Towers? It'll be just like old times.'

I want to scream. As the trees close in over the roof of the van and he steers along the narrow leaf-strewn lane, I consider opening the door and throwing myself out. But before I can move, he has parked behind that familiar copse of trees, and he is leaning over me.

'There now,' he says, and I can smell Coca-Cola and Juicy Fruit on his breath. 'Everything is back to normal. Did you miss me?'

As he debases me, I am certain I want to die.

The Plan

As if there has never been any break from it, life returns to the same rhythm as before. If Batty thinks me and Mary have talked about what he has done, he never says anything to me about it. He must have thought that he had gotten away with it.

The abuse resumes, a regular weekend occurrence during school time and a daily one over the holidays.

As my sixteenth birthday approaches, something in me snaps.

Sixteen is a milestone age, seen by many as the first step into adulthood. A lot of my friends leave school and start work at that age, and I even know young people who leave home and strike out on their own shortly after their sixteenth birthdays.

I don't want to leave the schoolhouse (not the one where I study or the one where I live), but I grasp the reality that, if I am going to get out of the dire situation I am in, there is only one person who is going to make it happen, and that is the person staring back at me when I look in the mirror.

The plan to get Batty out of my life (or as much out of my life as I reasonably can) involves a three-pronged approach:

1. **Bringing out my inner teenager:** up to this point I have always been an obliging and compliant teen. I do what I am told, keep to my curfews and spend virtually every weekend at my sister's home, working for very little pay to help her out. I *never* complain about this. I have seen friends have blazing rows with their parents, and I am well aware that a lot of my pals break rules left, right and centre. Even though it upsets me to have to do it (in truth, I worship my mam and dad and really don't want to make them angry), I know I have to start acting out. The next time I am ordered to go to Tallow to help Tisha, I plan to throw my first tantrum and refuse to go. I reason that it might not work the first time, or possibly even the second, but repeated strops will surely bear fruit sooner or later.

2. **Having a reason not to go:** the second strand of my plan is to play up to the things I know my parents like and appreciate – I will appeal to their better natures. When I was younger, I was a very successful Irish dancer. I am aware that a lot of dancing groups are away most weekends at competitions, tournaments and Irish music festivals and that, if I am involved with one of them, I will have a valid and incontrovertible reason not to go to Tallow. And this is a pursuit Daddy will be all too happy to support.

3. **Getting a boyfriend:** this is the toughest one, but something tells me that if I can gain the affections of one of the slightly older lads from our area, Batty will back off for fear I will tell on him and he might receive a hiding. I have no real wish to have a young man, but if I am to dissuade my brother-in-law from his pursuit of me, there seems no other option.

I put the plan into action right away.

Friday evenings are soon beset by rows in the Hickey household as I loudly proclaim that I *do not want to go to Tallow! It's boring,* I complain to my mother. *I want to stay here and hang out with my friends!* I do not try to hide my reluctance from Batty, and when I am sent out to the van by my furious mother, I sit hunched over in a sulk – to my surprise, he doesn't seem inclined to try anything with me when I am in a temper.

Looking back, I know I had found Batty's Achilles heel: he

was actually quite frightened of women. It seems that he did not know how to deal with an angry woman, including me.

I have learned that this is not unusual in sexual predators. From reading and examining other cases, I have found that a lot of them seem to have had difficult relationships with their mothers and are acting out of anger and dominance. Batty Prendergast could be powerful and frightening, but when I turned my own fury on him, he folded like a little boy.

The Irish dancing is easy. I ask one of the girls in my class in school, who I know is a champion dancer, about joining her group, and she is more than happy to bring me along. I tell Daddy about it, and he just glows with delight. Before I know it, I am going to rehearsals two evenings a week and am away dancing most Saturdays and a lot of Sundays, too. Batty still arrives with a hang-dog expression on Friday evenings, saying that Tisha really needs the help, but Daddy seems more than happy to tell him I am otherwise engaged.

One evening I am doing a dance recital for the Ballymacarbery youth club. One of the youth club members is called John. After my friends and I have danced, he comes over to chat. He is gentle and funny, and when he asks me if I will be going to the youth club disco that Friday night, I tell him I should be happy to attend, so long as he will be there.

We have fun at the disco and slow dance, and it is all very innocent. But within a week, I understand that John and I are going out.

Do you want to know something strange?

My plan worked. But I have no memory of the last time Batty Prendergast placed his hands on me. I had thought it would be huge and dramatic and the world would stop turning, but that didn't happen. I think what occurred was that I asserted myself – I projected my identity and some kind of inner strength, and it scared him.

I should have been over the moon, full of piss and vinegar and the power of my own self-importance. Only I wasn't.

I was grappling with a whole new set of problems.

CENTRAL CRIMINAL COURT, DUBLIN

AUGUST 2018

Guilty!

You've probably been wondering why Batty Prendergast decided to change his plea to guilty. This man, who has showed no remorse whatsoever throughout the proceedings, who sat unmoved while the charges against him were read out, suddenly decides to do the right thing.

It seems very out of character, doesn't it?

I learned after court was finished on that second day that Batty was given no choice.

The barristers for the DPP told me that the evidence was mounting against him, and it was pointed out in the strongest terms to him that by continuing to protest his innocence Batty would be looking at a much heavier sentence.

You have to remember that both me and Deedee were bringing charges. We had given statements, and everyone who was mentioned in those statements as knowing about the abuse had been interviewed by the police and subsequently given their own statements. Noel Whelan, the barrister for the DPP, told me that my account and that of John (who, God bless him, had spoken to David Mansfield and then returned *twice more* to give further information he remembered) *and* that of other witnesses all matched up beautifully. The details of these three statements alone, given by people who had had no dealings with one another for years, all tallied. They could not have been made up.

Now consider that the accounts of abuse provided by myself and Deedee, along with that of Mary (who has decided not to add her testimony to the case), also corresponded closely. The barristers were very clear that the evidence, circumstantial as it was and relating to events going back more than thirty years, all combined to reveal a picture of a serial abuser, a dangerous sexual predator with a clearly defined strategy for grooming families and a set of often-used locations to bring his underage victims to (Lismore Towers, for instance, showed up more than once in victim testimony).

By pleading guilty, Batty was not trying to alleviate the suffering of those of us he had harmed. He wasn't trying to lessen the pain of his wife or his children. He was saving his own skin. This was another instance of his finely tuned survivor instinct kicking in. He was cornered, and this was the only way he was going to help himself.

Add to this the decision by Justice Creedon not to split the cases (which was also, I have been told, because their details were so similar) and Batty could have been looking at some serious jail time.

It took me months to understand that this was down to the power of the truth. I had been running from the shadows in my life for so long, I had forgotten truth was on my side. Over the years I buried my pain, thinking no one would believe me or care about my suffering.

Yet when I started to tell, and when other people Batty had hurt stepped up and spoke their truths too, the power of our message was undeniable. And that power was stronger than the evil Batty Prendergast had done.

Isn't that a beautiful thing to be able to say?

Truth won.

It doesn't always, but it did this time.

On the Stand

I walk up to the witness stand to give my victim impact statement. Everything is moving in slow motion. I am wearing heels and am terrified I will trip over and make an idiot of myself in front of everyone. The stand looks to be absurdly far away, and for an awful moment I am convinced I will never get there.

But then, in a blink, I am sitting down and the whole court is before me and I fix the microphone and pull my chair in – it is like someone else is doing these things, but I trust that instinct and a drive for survival will get me through.

I look at the text on the pages I have brought with me – I have spent hours preparing this, poring over each word, trying to make sure the statement will articulate everything

I need to say. I have waited years for this, and I am not going to allow anything to lessen the power of this moment.

For a terrible, indeterminate, lurching expanse of time the words jump and leap and swim before me, and I have to swallow and take deep breaths. My best friend from back home, Deirdre, who used to play tennis with me and go for bike rides into the mountains, has given me a stone, a talisman to give me strength – it is a token of the love and closeness we have had for so many years, and now I squeeze it and take stock of the fact that, no matter how it feels, I am not alone.

The stone is flat and smooth and grey, and in black letters Deirdre has written the word *Strength* on it.

When we were children, on the long winter nights, Deirdre would walk with me to halfway between our two houses – it was a point called Christy Hallinane's Gate. We would part company there and each make for our separate homes, and when we arrived we would call out to one another: 'I'm home!'

We made a vow that neither of us would go inside until we were sure the other was safe.

Now, in this moment of great darkness, as I squeeze the stone, I feel her reaching out for me, waiting for me to tell her I am safe home.

The only way to get home safe is to get through this statement.

I start to read.

'Today,' I begin, 'I take my life back. I am so glad to get

this day, to be able to stand here in front of my family and friends and say what I've wanted to say for years.'

I pause and take a breath. I will not break down and start crying. Every single syllable must be heard and understood.

The judge looks at me with concern. 'There's a glass of water in front of you, Ms Hickey,' she says. 'Take your time. We are all here at your disposal.'

I take a sip and continue.

'Batty Prendergast,' I say, turning to look at him, 'as my life starts at this moment, yours ends lonely and miserable, which is just what you deserve. You can never hurt anyone again, and from this I take great peace.'

My brother-in-law, my abuser, the monster that haunted my dreams for more than thirty years, continues to stare at me, unblinking and seemingly unmoved. I don't care. He has taken so much but he won't take this moment as well.

'Bartholomew Prendergast,' I say his name slowly, pronouncing each syllable, 'I have won.'

Those three words explode from me like a battle cry. There have been so many times when I thought nothing good would ever come my way, when the world seemed to only want to beat me down.

It is a sweet moment, but it doesn't last. The worst part of this whole awful process is about to begin.

I just don't know it yet.

WEST WATERFORD

THE 1980S

John

God love him, but he learns fast that being my boyfriend isn't going to be easy.

On the first night at the youth club disco, he goes to kiss me when we're dancing the slow set. During 'I Want to Know What Love Is' by Foreigner, he leans down and goes in for a smooch.

Now, I am inexperienced when it comes to real, healthy relationships, but I'm not blind and I'm not stupid. I have been to teen discos and I have witnessed what goes on when the DJ declares that he is going to 'slow it down'. It is a code word for making out.

I like John. I might even (somewhere underneath all the confusion) fancy him a bit. But there is just no way I am going to allow him to put me in the position Batty

Prendergast did, where I am going to be pressured into performing all kinds of sick sex acts on him. When he puts his lips against mine, I give him a quick, friendly peck and move my head out of range.

A fortnight later we are walking from the shop in Ballymacarbery back to John's house, and he suggests we take a stroll in the pinewoods nearby. As happens with young people, we start cuddling and he (gently) tries to move things a little further.

And I get upset.

Tears come, and not a little anger, and I push him away and stalk off. John is confused, but he does not get annoyed. He tells me everything is fine and suggests we go on to his house where we can watch TV with his family.

Gratefully, I agree, and the moment passes.

A few days later we are alone and I sense it coming again. Before he can even make a move, I bolt. That becomes my way of dealing with it: as soon as I see the signals that John wants to get physically intimate, I make my excuses and get out of there. If a hug becomes too erotic, I push away or feign illness.

I know this is difficult for him and must be deeply frustrating, but he is such a nice guy, so protective and caring, he tolerates it without complaint. I am aware that I'm being unfair, and probably quite cruel, but for the first month or so I don't know any other way of coping.

One evening I am at his house and a phone call comes from my mother.

Batty and Tisha have had a baby by now, and they want me to babysit that night, which of course means sleeping over. I am non-committal (I can't really throw one of my trademark strops in front of John's parents), but as soon as the call ends, it's obvious something is wrong. I decide to go out on a limb; this young man has already shown countless times that he can be trusted. He has asked nothing of me other than friendship and has treated me incredibly sweetly, in spite of my sending such mixed signals.

I tell him. I don't go into the gory details, but I share enough so that John is in no doubt that I am afraid of my brother-in-law and that I have good reason to be.

'I just don't want to go,' I sob. 'I've done everything I can to stop my family sending me over there, but how the hell am I going to get out of this one?'

John looks at me with such concern on his face, my heart almost breaks for him.

'I'll go with you,' he says.

'You can't do that!' I can hardly believe what I'm hearing. 'They'd never let you sleep over!'

'I don't have to,' he says. 'I'll bring you over on my bike and drive us both home afterwards.'

John has a motorbike that I admire greatly but have never been on, as my mother has made me swear not to so much as stand next to it without all the proper safety gear.

'You know I can't go on the bike.' I sigh.

'I was saving this for the weekend,' he says with a grin, 'but now seems as good a time as any.'

He goes out to the hall and returns with a large cardboard box. Inside is a brand-new helmet, leathers, boots and gloves: an entire set of gear, all in my size. 'Do you think this will keep your mother happy?'

Laughing and crying all at once, I throw my arms around him, thanking him from the bottom of my heart.

Batty's face is a picture when the two of us arrive in Tallow later that evening. I can tell he is shocked to his core, but (survivor that he is) he recovers quickly and lavishes charm and attention on to John.

I tend to think of that evening as the official end of my abuse at the hands of Batty Prendergast. Even though the last incident was before it, the threat was always present until John offered to go to Tallow with me. That simple gesture of solidarity, friendship and love closed one of the most awful chapters of my life.

I will be grateful to that kind-hearted young man until my dying day.

Philip

I'd love to be able to tell you that John and I made a go of it, but you have probably already worked out that isn't on the cards. I know he is madly in love with me, but as the months pass, I am certain it isn't going to last.

He goes out of his way to make sure I am OK – he can't do enough for me – but within a few months I am feeling smothered and irritated by him.

To be absolutely clear, this is a textbook case of 'it's not him, it's me'. John is, I believe, one of the nicest, kindest, most decent people ever to come into my life. I am simply too damaged and mixed up to appreciate him at the moment he enters the story, and after about six months, I split up with him.

I know that I am breaking his heart, but at the time I

believe I am doing what is right for both of us. Had I stayed with him, we would have both ended up miserable.

For the next few years, I focus on my female friends, spending time with them and doing lots of dancing. Then, one evening I am in Dunne's pub in Touraneena when a group of young men arrive. I know most of them, as they are all seasonal workers, come to do various jobs on some of the larger farms in the Nire area.

One of them in particular stands out. He is tall and broad, with a full head of shaggy dark hair, the blue shadow of a beard always visible on his jawline, even just after he has shaved. He speaks in a thick Donegal accent that seems incredibly exotic in west Waterford, and I am drawn to him right away, despite my intention to keep out of relationships with guys for as long as I can.

His name is Philip, and no matter how hard I fight it, I know I am falling for him hopelessly.

Part of it is purely primal: he is strong and handsome and intensely masculine. I know this young man can handle himself, and I see the others in his group treat him as someone who is knowledgeable and capable, and I cannot help but admire that. When he speaks, people listen, and when he goes into a pub or a shop, all eyes are drawn to him right away.

He has charisma. It is a rough and ready and slightly dangerous charisma, but there is no denying that it is there.

There is another aspect to my desire for him that is more selfish. When I'm not going out with someone, the requests for me to go over to Tallow to babysit or help out in the salon become more insistent. I avoided it for the most part, and on the couple of occasions where I had no option, I managed to persuade one of my girlfriends to come with me, but I know that sooner or later I'm going to be forced to go over there alone, and then I will be at my brother-in-law's mercy.

I strongly feel that Philip will protect me. Thinking of him standing beside Batty gives me a thrill, as the older man seems so soft and weak in comparison.

We start going out, and I come to believe that this wild northern soul is the man who can really save me – from Batty and from the darkness inside myself. He makes me feel better about who I am. Even the sexual side of the relationship is easier with him – there is such an abandon in his sexuality that everything that has gone before doesn't seem to matter.

Once a month we travel on the train and bus to Donegal to visit his family, and I fall in love with the sparse, moor-like mountains where he is from. This place is so like the Comeraghs and yet so utterly different. I am made to feel very welcome by his people, and I learn their songs and their stories, and for the first time in my life I can see myself living somewhere other than Touraneena and the Nire.

I believe, now, that my relationship with Philip was all about escape. A man from about as far away as you can get (in a country as small as Ireland) walks in through the door of my local pub and I grab hold of him with both hands. Here is someone who can take me right away from all the pain that has come to inhabit my life. Here is a way out.

I don't fall pregnant on purpose.

But it means there is no option but to get married.

All we have to do is tell my parents.

Bonds of Love

When I find out I am pregnant at twenty years of age, Philip is characteristically strong and forceful about it.

'That's all right!' he says, picking me up in one of his rib-cracking bear-hugs. 'You don't need to worry – I'll stand by you and we'll get married and we'll have a marvellous life.'

I laugh at this, maybe a little bit hysterically.

'Sure, isn't it a good thing? Bringin' a wee one into the world can't be bad, can it?' he asks.

I wonder if my parents will agree with these sentiments.

I ask my mother if Philip can come over for dinner the following night. If this needs to be done, I tell myself, it's better to get it done quickly. After the meal we sit around the kitchen table, the women sipping mugs of tea while my father pours glasses of whiskey for him and Philip.

'Mammy, Daddy: Philip and I have something we want to tell you.'

I know what they're both thinking – it is the week before my twenty-first birthday, so I'm not unusually young to get engaged.

'Now, I know you're going to be a bit upset, but we've both talked this over and we know what we're doing—'

'You're pregnant, aren't you?' Mammy says before I can get another word out.

'Yes, but we're going to get married,' I protest, but it's too late.

'You have brought shame on this family,' my father says, and there are tears in his eyes. 'My God, Stephanie, what will they say in the church? What will our neighbours think?'

'You were not reared to behave like this,' my mother says, wringing her hands in anguish.

'Let's go,' Philip says, knocking back the whiskey in his glass and standing. 'I'm buggered if I'm gonna sit around and listen to this.'

'Don't you come back!' my father calls after us. 'You are not welcome here, neither of you!'

'I wouldn't dream of darkenin' your door again, ye miserable old goat!' Philip calls back as he drags me out the front door.

We begin the walk back to Tierney's, where he is farm manager.

'Well, I think that went well,' he says after we've put half a mile between us and them.

We both burst out laughing, which for me turns to tears just as quickly.

Upsetting my parents, causing them such pain, breaks my heart. To have them shun me is about the worst thing to ever happen, as far as I'm concerned. It never occurs to me to tell them that I am an adult and my own person, and therefore capable of making my own decisions. The abuse seems to have locked me, psychologically, at about the age of thirteen, and I still consult my parents on each and every decision.

Not any more.

Suddenly I am cut loose, and the world seems an even more frightening place than before.

I wonder if Philip really can protect me after all.

How To Tarnish a
Shotgun Wedding

Philip and I are married on 25 July 1992.

It is, to use a well-worn phrase, a shotgun wedding, although my husband-to-be and I are the ones wielding the weapon – my parents are still not really talking to us, and we do all the planning and preparation by ourselves, with little support.

I already know that the long-term plan is to move to Donegal. Philip's work in the Nire is seasonal and I have none at all. I am aware that he is getting itchy feet anyway, longing to return home to people who seem far less concerned with our scandalous union. I don't blame him. What started out as love's young dream has soured quickly.

It seems half the parish knows I'm pregnant and I am fed up of the judgement and shame I sense everywhere I go.

We're broke. What little money we have is being set aside for the deposit on a small house in Donegal, which means the wedding will be a tiny affair – just the two families – and we manage to scrape together the cost of a meal for everyone in the Park Hotel in Dungarvan.

I am trying to make the best of a bad lot. This is not how I dreamed of getting married, but I love Philip, and I am looking forward to being a mother, and we are both determined that we will have a good life together. I want the wedding to be a positive start to that. Small as it will be, it doesn't mean it can't be a joyful occasion.

The week before the happy day, I get a call from Tisha.

'I'm going to break with tradition and tell you what your wedding present is in advance,' she informs me.

'Go on then.' I laugh.

'Batty is going to be your wedding photographer.'

I feel the world constricting and I can't breathe.

'You don't need to thank me,' she carries on. 'It was his idea. He's always had a soft spot for you. Batty's a wonderful photographer. He'll do an amazing job.'

I want to scream at her that this is insane, shout that this man is not even welcome at my wedding, my special day. Doesn't she understand that this is supposed to be about the creation of a new family, one that he isn't a part of? Surely she knows we're going to be setting up our home hundreds of miles away, right at the other end of the country, where he can't get at us? As she continues to witter away down the phone, I have a vision of myself at the altar in Touraneena church, Philip beside me. Standing right next to the priest in his skin-tight jeans, an expensive camera slung about his neck, his erection prominent through the stone-washed denim, is Batty Prendergast, leering down at me.

I want to vomit.

Philip knows about Batty. When I told my fiancé, he wanted to go right over to Tallow and confront him – Philip was, in fact, hellbent on beating the living daylights out of him. I begged my future husband to just play the game. Things were already bad with my parents, and I didn't want to cause another scene. It was tough for Philip, a man who rarely bottled up his feelings and was inclined to express anger with the same enthusiasm he did joy, to sit quietly and be polite when we were forced to spend time in Batty's company, and I know having him as our wedding photographer must be killing Philip as much as it is me.

But sure, it's just one day.

One special day.

The weather is not great when the twenty-fifth dawns, and Batty takes very few shots around the church. Philip looks dashing in his suit, and I have a modest (and I think quite beautiful) dress – my pregnancy is in the very early stages (we're just a couple of months in), so I'm still slim. In fact, I think I look lovely. My brother-in-law takes a couple of shots of us exchanging the rings and some of us signing the register, and then, to my delight, he disappears. Tisha actually asks where he's gone, but I take it as a sign that maybe the gods of weddings are taking care of me after all.

We arrive in Dungarvan and, to my horror, Batty is standing at the door of the hotel, and he grabs me right away. 'I want to get a few shots of you on your own,' he says.

This is normal, I tell myself. I'll want these pictures for my album. It'll be good.

Batty leads me to a table on the lawn outside the hotel's lobby and sits me down. He leans in close, tilting my head to the left. He smells of Brut, Polo mints and red lemonade.

'Pretend you're looking at the man of your dreams,' he says, then winks. 'And I'll be standing right over here!'

I make a pretend laugh, but inside I'm cringing.

'You look gorgeous, Stephanie,' he says, and I hear the familiar grind of lust in his voice.

I know he is undressing me with his eyes, but there is nothing I can do but go along with it. He takes photograph after photograph, and he uses every available opportunity to put his hands on me, moving my arm this way, putting his hands on my waist to point me this direction or that.

When I finally get the album, there are four shots of me and Philip. All the rest are of me on my own. I can't believe no one noticed he was taking so few of us as a couple, but this is part of how Batty operates – he is nothing if not subtle. He *seemed* to be taking loads of us. But he wasn't. It was all about me. Me and him. If I didn't know better, I would call the album a love letter.

But I do know better. It is a message that he is still watching me, that no matter what my marital status, I'm still his.

The final blow of the day comes after the meal. Philip and I have booked a band to play, as the hotel has said we can have use of the room all evening so long as we can guarantee they'll make their money from drinks sold. As the staff push back tables, I notice the man who plays drums with Batty's band, Stardust, coming in carrying some cases.

'What's going on?' I ask Tisha.

'It's another present for you.' My sister grins.

'I don't understand.'

'Batty swopped gigs with the crowd you'd booked – he says they're not that great. He's going to play tonight, and they'll fill in for his band another time.'

'You mean ...?' I splutter.

'That's right – Batty Prendergast is going to provide the music for your wedding!' Tisha beams. 'He says he couldn't let it pass without performing for you!'

I don't dance much that night. I sit in the dark and watch as Batty wiggles his chunky hips and strikes power poses on the stage. I cannot believe it is happening. My abuser has, literally, taken over my wedding day.

As I lie in bed later that night and my new husband snores loudly in my ear, I wonder if I will ever be free of him.

A Promise Kept

I think Philip actually enjoyed the day, and the guests all seemed to have a marvellous time (whatever kind of human being Batty is, he knows how to lead a band and he had the whole place jumping), but to me it stands out as one of the lowest moments of my life.

Luckily, I don't have much time to dwell on it.

I give birth to a beautiful nine-pound baby girl in December and name her Danielle. She is healthy, content and has her father's dark hair and soulful eyes. She makes me very happy, and Philip dotes on her.

But there are clouds on the horizon.

My new husband's father is very ill, and Philip has made it clear he wants to return home to Donegal as soon as we can. I am happy to go. I did not think I would ever want to leave the Nire, but all the joy has been taken out of the place for me. I have come to believe the only way I can truly be free, truly be myself, is to get as far away as I can.

But I want the people I love to know *why* I am going.

My relationship with Mammy and Daddy is still in tatters due to my pregnancy, so telling them is not really an option. And I can't tell Tisha.

Shortly before Philip and I move to Donegal, I am in Dunford's pub playing pool with Ciaran, Deedee's boyfriend.

Ciaran and Deedee have been together since she was sixteen. Because his parents died when he was very young, Ciaran has lived with my family for years, and he is as much like a brother to me as Michael or Richard is.

I'm in a funny mood, still upset over the bizarre twist my wedding took.

Ciaran takes a shot and steps back, pondering the layout of the balls.

'Ciaran, I want to tell you something,' I say all of a sudden.

'All right, but can I take this shot first?' He goes for a corner pocket and misses. 'OK, I'm ready now,' he says.

I know he will always support me, that nothing I can say will stop him loving me. But his response is still a shock.

When I am finished talking, he puts his arms around me, tears wet on his cheeks, and says: 'He did it to Deedee, too.'

My reaction to this news is one I have thought about a lot over the years. I don't know whether it shows me in a good light or not, but I'm going to tell you, for better or worse.

Initially I feel sick and empty – Deedee is someone I look up to (she is almost a hero to me). To think she has had to endure the lascivious attentions of this awful man causes me great pain. I want to scream.

But a part of me also feels relief. Knowing Batty had abused my friend Mary is dreadful, but Mary is not a member of my family. I always believed I had been singled out. Now I know I was not.

I am not alone. It almost feels good.

I am not proud of it, but there it is.

The following day, my sister and I go for a walk in the pinewoods and we hold each other and cry and promise we will never allow the other to be hurt by Batty again. Deedee wants to go to the police, but, to my shame, I beg her not to.

I am starting out in life, my marriage is new and I have a baby and I am finally going to be away from Batty and his poison.

'Please, Deedee,' I say. 'I don't want anyone to know. I couldn't cope with it.'

And there, in the long shadows of the trees, my big sister promises to wait until I am ready.

To her credit, it is a promise she keeps for twenty-five years.

The Homes of Donegal

Things are not good in my marriage before we move to Donegal. I pretend they are (to myself as much as anyone else) and I try to project a sense that we are the perfect little family, living on the farm that Philip manages, but the truth is very different.

As soon as we decide we are definitely moving to Ballyshannon, Philip's home place, my husband changes and so do I. He goes from being an attentive (if always a little wild) partner who is always there when I need him to a much more distant person. I know he is very focused on returning to his family and re-establishing his life in his old haunts, but it is hard for me to cope with. And, despite myself, I become even more needy in response.

Discussing it causes a row. So we both say nothing.

The move to Donegal is getting closer, and I don't want us to go through the stress and difficulty of such an upheaval while at each other's throats. One evening, I cook Philip dinner, buy as expensive a bottle of wine as I can afford and sit him down for a chat.

I tell him I love him, that I want the marriage to work and that I believe we can be happy in the north. I don't want to stop him from seeing his friends, and as long as we have the rent paid and food on the table, I am happy for him to have a few pints if he wishes. I just need him to talk to me and let me know what he is doing and what his movements will be. We are supposed to be a partnership.

We go to bed that night feeling closer than we have in many weeks.

A month later, I move from one end of Ireland to the other.

The house in Donegal is near the beach, overlooking the ocean. It could not be more different to the Nire, but I love it nonetheless and try to make our home beautiful and welcoming. Now that I am a permanent resident, Philip's family make less of a fuss of me, which is natural, and I spend long hours on my own with Danielle, as Philip works during the day and helps care for his father, who is dying of cancer, in the evenings.

I try to make friends with some of the locals, but they don't seem as open as the people of Touraneena. Maybe they are friendlier than I am giving them credit for, but there seems to be one barrier I can't overcome – I am eternally a blow-in.

I focus on being a wife and mother instead.

We have two more children: Philip Jr and Dylan.

Philip's father grows weaker and weaker, and this is another loss, as he has been a good friend to me – he has always told his son that I should be his number one priority and to treat me like a princess.

When the old man dies, it feels like my last ally in Donegal is gone.

The Last Straw

Philip has started staying out all night. Looking back, I don't blame him because, as he has become more distant, I have become more angry and cold.

The days where I tell myself he is playing cards or watching DVDs are long past. I sit up all night when he is away, brooding, convinced he is having an affair – I have no reason to believe such a thing, but my head is a swirling maelstrom of paranoia and anguish.

I create all kinds of scenarios in my head. Maybe it's a regular girl, someone he works with, or maybe it's one-night stands. Philip is good looking by any standards, and on the rare nights we go out together, I see the way women leer at him. I've stood there like an eejit while they chat him up, not even bothered that I'm right beside him.

Sure, why would they be? I'm the skinny blow-in from Waterford who can't even keep her man happy. Why in the name of God would anyone be intimidated by me?

After I put the children to bed at night, I sit up and gaze out at the rolling, roiling sea and I cry. Speaking aloud to the night-time sky, I list everything that I have lost, and the litany seems to go on forever.

One night in December I have had enough. He has not come home again and it is three o'clock in the morning and I go a little bit mad. In spite of the hour, I call every number in my diary until I track him down – Philip is in his first cousin's house. I wrap the children in blankets and woolly hats, pack them in their car-seats and drive over there.

The house is full of people and music is blaring loudly. I find Philip in the kitchen. He is with his friends – there is not another woman in sight. I realise I have been paranoid, but I'm too angry to care. All the bitterness and loneliness pours out, and as it does our marriage dies. Looking on this scene with the eyes of a much older, wiser woman, I understand now that I was shouting at Batty, at my parents, probably even at myself.

I do not remember what is said, but I know that it is full of the hurt and anger and disappointment I have been feeling for the past ten years, ever since the shadows gathered and my childhood was taken away by someone I trusted.

My husband sits and takes my fury with characteristic stoicism – I might as well be screaming at a brick wall. Which makes me even angrier.

Philip's cousin tries to appease me, but I am inconsolable and pumped up with rage.

'You can keep him!' I scream as I stalk back out to the car and my sleeping children, the only good things I have left.

I drive back to the house – our marital home – and pack up all his things.

Maybe, I think, as I throw his clothes into black bin-liners, maybe there is something wrong with me.

Maybe I am not built to be happy.

The Wilderness Years

Philip and I negotiate our separation after five years of marriage without involving lawyers. It is not what I would call civil but neither does he put up much of a fight.

He agrees to having the children one evening a week and every second weekend. This means I cannot go back to the Nire, as it will interfere with his access and visitation. I'm still not really talking to my parents, anyway, so not being able to return home makes very little difference. I remain an exile, a southerner set adrift in the north.

I have moved from being trapped in my life in Waterford to being thoroughly excluded from it.

I become a living zombie. The only emotion I can register is sadness. I do not want to eat and what little weight I have drops from me rapidly. I try not to cry in front of the children, but as soon as they are out the door to school or in bed for the night, I allow the tears to flow freely. It gets to the point where I barely notice that I am weeping. It seems to be my natural state.

I believe that I am a failure. I came to this strange and beautiful place to build a happy life for me, my husband and my children. All I have succeeded in doing is destroying what joy there was and replacing it with despair. I have no friends, no family and no hope.

I am as alone as I have ever been.

The only human contact I receive occurs when I am handing over the children, but even that is fraught. There are weekends when Philip does not show up. There is no warning, no excuse – he just doesn't arrive.

On other occasions he sends his mother to collect Danielle, Dylan and Philip Jr.

I want to tell her I am sorry, that I would take it all back if I could, but I know it is far too late for that. When the children are away from me, I am utterly bereft – they are the only comfort I have – and I walk the beach in the dwindling evening light thinking how easy it would be to wade out into the grey waves, never to be seen again.

If I was not convinced the children needed me, I would have done it without a moment of hesitation. Their simple, innocent love saved my life.

One morning, six years after I moved to Donegal, there is a knock on my door and to my huge surprise my mother is standing there. Things have not been good since I told her about my unexpected pre-marital pregnancy but here she stands, her arms weighed down by bags of groceries. She has made the trip up on the train and bus from Waterford. Without a word, she walks past me, places the groceries on the kitchen table and (in a very uncharacteristic act) takes me in her arms. She says nothing, but I don't need her to. Her unexpected presence is enough.

She sits me down and makes us both tea, producing some homemade scones that she slathers with butter and jam.

'Now,' she says when we are both seated, 'tell me all about it.'

And she and I talk with an openness and honesty I do not think we have ever shared before. I tell her how lost I feel and how alone and I beg for her forgiveness for the shame I have brought upon her. She shushes me and tells me that is all in the past. What matters now is that she is here and I am her daughter and her grandchildren need to be thought of and we must put our heads together and fix what has gone wrong.

'You might feel as if you are alone,' she says, 'but you are not. You have a home and a family, and we might get angry with one another from time to time, but we never stop loving. You must not forget that.'

She comes to visit every fortnight after that, always with a parcel of food and other odds and ends I might need. Now there has been a reconciliation, I drive home to visit on the weekends Philip is not due to have the children.

I do this for four years.

Then one day my husband announces he is going away to work again.

I don't query his decision. All I know is that if Philip is choosing not to be in Donegal, he cannot have access visits, and that means I am no longer legally bound to stay. I pack what I can fit into my car and leave what I can't behind.

I feel as if a massive weight has been lifted from me. It is almost like I am floating.

'We are going home,' I tell my children as that windswept strand disappears in the rearview mirror.

I am almost thirty years old.

Soulmates

Once my marriage breaks down, I am determined never to be in a relationship again. Men, as far as I am concerned, are all the same: they are only about taking.

When I arrive back in Touraneena after my years in Donegal, all I want is to be left alone to look after my kids, and the only kind of relationship I am interested in is with my female friends. I happily rekindle my bond with Deirdre and look forward to going out for a few drinks with friends at the end of each week.

I live for a few weeks in the schoolhouse with my parents, and then I get a house six miles away, on a hill overlooking the Comeraghs. I secure a job delivering meals for a catering company, and with some money in my pocket and the support of my family again, I feel reborn.

I see Tisha every now and then when she visits my mother, and Batty only rarely – if he does happen to arrive over to my parents' house for a visit, I make an excuse and leave. I make a conscious decision not to think about the shadows and darkness of the past. A part of me knows it poisoned my marriage and I do not want it to do any further harm.

The next few years are happy ones as I rebuild myself slowly and delicately, learning to trust the world as a place where happiness can be experienced if you are open to it.

One evening, about four years after I return to west Waterford, I am in O'Keefe's pub with friends when some guys I know come in. In their company is a dark-skinned, strongly built man with close-cropped hair whom I have not met before. Something about him is very different, and it takes me a while to recognise that he is Italian, with quite limited English.

Later I meet him in the smoking area, and he comes over to introduce himself. 'What is you name?' he asks me.

'I'm Stephanie,' I say, extending my hand to shake.

'I am Angelo,' he says, and instead of taking my hand, he bows with a flourish.

I laugh at that.

'Please to let me buy you a drink,' he offers. 'It would be my pleasure to do this.'

'Thank you, but I have a drink already,' I say. 'You are very kind, but no.'

'I only want to be friend, to talk with you,' he says. 'I am not chat you up.'

'I have to go back to my friends,' I say and, smiling, I head back to the bar.

Remember I told you before about my gut, and how I am used to sensing when men are being dangerous? Well, my gut is talking to me this evening, and every bit of it tells me this is a good man. His manner is completely unlike anyone I have ever met – it is almost like he knows that I am delicate and have had tough experiences. He is doing everything he can to make me see that he is safe and kind and will not do anything I don't want him to.

But I am afraid. He is strange and foreign and I just don't want to put myself out there yet. I'm not ready.

I see him many times over the coming months. I walk home from the pub most Friday nights (it is a short stroll through well-lit areas) and Angelo often passes me in his car and will always stop to offer me a lift, which I good-naturedly decline. He never forces the issue, and this routine – him slowing down to drive along beside me for a few moments while he gracefully offers to drive me the rest of the way home, me politely turning his offer down – has, without either of us realising it, become one of the building blocks of our relationship. It is a kind of dance.

Six months later I am in the Arms Hotel in Dungarvan. I have just had a wisdom tooth out and am trying to numb the pain with hot whiskeys. I leave my friends to go for a smoke, and who should stroll out to have a cigarette but

Angelo. He grins and we try to chat. His English is still terrible, but he is so expressive and such a good mime that we never have a problem understanding one another.

He finishes his cigarette and is about to go back to his friends (he is playing poker in the main bar) when I say: 'If you still want to drive me home, I could do with a lift this evening.'

A massive grin breaks across his face, and he gives me a thumbs-up. 'You find me when you ready, Stephanie,' he says. 'I will bring you then. OK?'

'OK,' I agree.

An hour later I find him at a table with a lot of other men, a large bundle of notes and coins in the middle of it all. I shyly pull a chair up beside Angelo and let him know I'm ready. Without pausing, he drops his hand of cards onto the table.

'I fold,' he says and reaches for his coat.

I don't know if this is true or not, but Bruno, his best friend, told me later that the hand Angelo threw away with such disregard would have won the pot. Like I said, that might just be a story, but I like to think it's true – it's kind of romantic!

We arrive at my door and I ask my new friend if he would like to come in.

'No, thank you,' he says.

'Are you sure?' I ask. 'I could make you a cup of coffee?'

'No. I will not go in, thank you,' he says. Once again, this is so unlike any man I have ever known. 'I make you this deal, though,' he says. 'You meet me tomorrow. Anywhere you like.'

I decide to be completely honest. 'I have three children,' I tell him. 'If you want to have a relationship with me, they will always come first. Always.'

'Three children?' he asks.

'Three, yes.'

'You want to meet at the playground, in the park?'

I almost laugh at him. 'Are you serious?'

'Yes. Bring you kids. For now, we be friends. If you kids like me, they can be friends too, eh?'

We meet the following afternoon. Danielle is twelve, Dylan almost eleven and Philip five. While all my instincts tell me Angelo is a sweet man, I am still on my guard – why would he ask me to bring my kids along? – but he treats them with the same courtesy and old-world politeness he does me, and does not so much as lay a finger on them without my permission (he lifts Dylan onto the monkey bars at one stage).

He is funny and nice and easy to be around. When we say our goodbyes (he does not overstay his welcome) we exchange phone numbers. He rings a couple of days later to ask me out but prefaces it by inquiring when it would be convenient for me to get a babysitter. He does not for a moment propose coming over to my house.

Once again, he makes me feel safe and at ease.

We go out several times. We have great fun and he is the perfect gentleman.

Only maybe he is too perfect.

I have never been out with a man who has not, even in the most subtle way, tried to put his hands on me. Angelo has not tried to hold my hand; he has not tried to kiss me goodnight; and he has not tried to put his arm around me.

By the fourth date, I am beginning to wonder if he might be gay.

And I feel bad about this, because it is actually a huge relief not to be fighting a bloke off all the time. But I am beginning to wonder.

The next time we go out, I decide it is time to tell him about my relationship history (not about Batty, but about Philip and my marriage). He tells me about coming to Ireland initially on holiday and loving it and deciding to come back to work in a restaurant. He has been married before, too, but it didn't work out and he has been divorced for years.

He is a bit older than me (I'm in my thirties at this stage; he's in his forties), and for the next few weeks we spend our dates slowly getting to know one another. I regularly invite him in when he drops me home, but he always refuses.

'I no want to be in your home with your children,' he says. 'They have been through enough, and you have been through enough. When you and I are sure, then we can be with your children too. For now, you learn about me and I learn about you.'

I now realise that one of my flaws was that I had always rushed into relationships. I had gone from zero to ninety miles an hour within the space of a few weeks. Angelo makes me slow things down and just explore the kind of relationship we both want to have. It is a year before he agrees to come into my home and really spend time with the children. Dylan falls for him right away – he is such a fatherly figure.

The first time we are intimate, he is so gentle and reassuring. I tell him I must have the lights out, and he just laughs. 'Lights on, lights off, is all good for me!'

My parents take to him (and he to them) remarkably quickly. I am incredibly relieved.

I fall pregnant with Riccardo and those nine months are the most blissful I can remember. We experience the whole pregnancy together and he is warm and supportive.

Here's the most important thing: Angelo makes my family complete. I always say that Ciaran is Deedee's soulmate, and I always aspired towards having a relationship like that. Now I do. I found my soulmate with Angelo. If I had not had him, I would not have been able to go through the trauma of the trial.

He was there for me every step of the way.

He still is.

CENTRAL CRIMINAL COURT, DUBLIN

AUGUST 2018

Deedee Takes the Stand

I sit back down after reading my victim impact statement and it feels as if the whole thing took place in a dream. I ask Angelo if I did OK, and he wraps his arms around me and tells me he is so proud.

'You read it slow, you read it carefully, I hear and understand every word,' he says.

It has been a big thing, deciding to read the victim impact statement myself, because most survivors don't – their lawyer reads it on their behalf because there is always the risk they will break down or make a mess of it, thereby diminishing the effectiveness of having it read into the record in the first place.

Mine, it seems, has been a success.

As Angelo and I are talking, it is announced that Deedee will now read her statement. I have no idea what she is going to say – I have not read her words and I am even more nervous for her than I was for myself.

Tisha and I have not spoken since I made the decision to press charges against Batty, so there has been silence between us now for more than two years. This has made my relationship with Deedee extremely important to me. She has been with me through all the challenges of bringing our cases to court, and I do not think I would have been able to do it without her.

She takes the stand and I can see she is just about keeping it together.

'I went from being a happy, innocent child to living in constant fear because of your abuse,' Deedee begins. 'I feel huge regret that I didn't speak out when it happened to me the first time, especially after learning that you were doing the same and worse to my younger sister.'

If you didn't know Deedee, you might think she is really coping well, but I know she is teetering on the brink of collapse. I want to run up and throw my arms around her and take her away from all this pain, but she has to come through the flames just as I did. I glance over and Batty might as well be asleep for all the emotion he is showing. Deedee looks at him too, and then she breaks down. The last part of her statement is read through tears.

'To think that I could have stopped her from experiencing that hurt,' Deedee continues, 'has been a constant source of guilt for me. The last few years have been horrendous. I do not believe I will ever shake off the shame that, if only I had spoken out at the time ... The fact that I am able to face you now across a courtroom gives me hope that I can finally move on.'

I want to cheer for Deedee as she walks down to her seat.

A third victim's statement is read into the record by the barrister. He explains that the victim was nine years old when the abuse began.

'I was abused when I was a young and vulnerable child,' the statement concludes. 'I was unable to defend myself. It took me a long time to realise I was not to blame, and that during the abuse I was paralysed by fear, which prevented me from kicking him in the testicles and running away.'

That strikes a chord with me, and I look over at Deedee and see she is thinking the same thing – I used to wonder why I didn't fight back. There were countless times I had him in positions where I could have done him serious damage, but I never took advantage.

'I used to worry that Batty might abuse his own daughter, and I wondered how his wife stayed with him, knowing she was married to a paedophile. It must have been a bitter pill for her to swallow.'

That line shocks me. I suppose we have all thought it, but this is the first time I have heard it spoken aloud. It evokes not so much as a flicker from Batty.

'I do not blame myself any more,' the statement ends. 'The

wheel has turned full circle. I just hope Batty Prendergast never puts the fear of God into a child again.'

The barrister puts the pages back into a folder, and all eyes turn to Justice Creedon.

She now has to talk to us about sentencing.

It's the bit we've all been waiting for – and we're going to have to wait a lot longer.

WEST WATERFORD
2014–2015

Being a Parent

I have four children: Danielle, Dylan, Philip and Riccardo.

I love them in ways I cannot really express. I know beyond any doubt that I would happily die for them, and I also know that what is more important is that I *live* for them.

There have been times, many times over the years, when being alive seemed more of a burden than I could endure, but in those times the faces of my children kept me going. When you love someone unconditionally and completely, the idea of hurting them is more than you can bear, and I knew that by taking my life I would be allowing Batty to win, and that would have damaged my beautiful kids irreparably.

I often wonder if I am the type of parent I am because of what happened to me growing up. I suppose I must be because we are the sum of all our experiences, aren't we?

The things I am going to admit now are not the most politically correct. You won't see people posting stuff like this on Facebook or Instagram, but let's be honest, you know so much personal stuff about me at this stage, we might as well get it all out on the table.

My parenting is flawed, and I know it.

I am an indulgent parent – I rarely force my kids to do things they don't want to do. I remember begging not to be sent to Tallow, and despite my protestations I was made to go. I told Bartholomew Prendergast 'no' more times than I can count, but he just ignored me. I won't put my kids through that, so if one of them tells me that they don't want to do something, I don't argue, even when I probably should.

I am an overly gentle parent, too. I don't like confrontation, and if my children are annoyed with me or raise their voices (as teens are inclined to do with regularity), I become upset and am liable to just give in and let them have whatever they want. I know this is wrong and is probably doing them no favours, but something in me finds the challenge difficult, and I cannot abide my kids being angry with me or not talking to me.

I wonder if this stems from the time when my parents cut me off when I moved up north. That sense of isolation and aloneness is still very raw in me. I am terrified of being back in that place again or putting my own children in that place.

Perhaps the biggest flaw in my parenting is rooted in my belief that I am not worthy of love. I find it hard to believe that my children love me the way I love them, even though they show me every single day that they do. I am so neurotic, some days I need constant reassurance. So when my kids act out (which, of course, they do because it is healthy and normal) I often interpret that as them telling me they don't love me and that I am failing as a mother.

I know this is ridiculous and selfish, but there you are. It is how I feel.

I am lucky that I have Angelo, who is so strong and reliable and is a steady hand and a constant presence. Deedee is always there, and so are my brothers.

I do my best. I am a good enough parent, most days.

I wake up every day and I tell myself I will do better, and a lot of days, I do.

On other occasions I seem to tread water, and on still others, I screw up and I am ashamed of myself.

But you know, one thing I never, ever doubt is how much I love my kids. As I told Angelo that first evening he dropped me home, all those years ago: they come first.

Taking to the Road

I'm forty-two years old and I feel like I have nothing in my life just for me and no one else.

I love my family, but sometimes it's like all I do is give, and while I know they love me, the voices inside my head are always there, telling me I'm not worthy of love and that people just put up with me out of politeness or simple habit.

I work in a couple of jobs, and on some days I even like them, but being a carer or chief cook and bottle-washer for a catering company just doesn't seem as fulfilling as it could be. It's like my life has become an endless drudge. I wake up in the morning and there are so many days where I don't want to get out of bed. I lie there and look at the ceiling while Angelo snores quietly beside me, and I tell myself to snap out of it, and after a time I drag myself upright and get dressed methodically, one leg at a time, one arm after the other.

I light a cigarette and I make tea and I sit at the kitchen table – the Comeraghs visible through the window – while Angelo and my children sleep, and try to still my stupid, chattering brain and force myself to get through today. It's kind of like being an alcoholic in recovery, only without the drink – I do it one day at a time, and that is as much as I can cope with. I can't think about tomorrow because that is just too scary. I'll deal with today, and that's enough of a mountain to climb.

Not thinking about the darkness, about Batty, isn't working any more. The pain still hits me. Sometimes, when I'm feeling really rough, there is anger and resentment – not just at him, but at everyone around me.

At the world in general.

Why did it happen to me? Even after thirty years I feel that I am worthless, so worthless that some fucking scumbag felt he had the right to use and abuse me. Why does everyone else get to have a beautiful, fumbling, glorious sexual awakening, one they can look back on and smile and maybe even tell their girlfriends about over glasses of wine, and mine has to be something out of a nightmare? Why do I not get to feel beautiful and desirable and special? Why is every single thing a fight?

On those days I bite my tongue, and people around me notice I've gone quiet and those who really know me give me a wide berth. I'm thankful for that. The anger scares me a little, not least because it would be so easy to turn it inwards.

The voices tell me that everyone would be better off if I wasn't around. My exhausted, tormented mind conjures up a sense of relief and elation at the cessation of my existence. It wouldn't take much to be free. It could be over quickly and easily and painlessly.

The universe would be a better place if I wasn't in it.

It takes a supreme effort not to allow these thoughts to take over everything. I cannot allow myself the luxury of even thinking that way – my kids need me and my parents need me and my dying would mean that he wins.

I've come too far for that.

In the dark hours of the night those voices tell me that he has already taken everything. When all the joy is gone out of your life, what have you got left? It would be a lie to say I feel like that all the time, but sometimes, it's like a crushing weight on top of me. I know I need something, that I have to find an outlet, a release. I'm scared that if I don't, all this poison will eat me up.

Then one day, out of the blue, my sister Deedee, who lives nearby, suggests I try running.

A group of women are starting a Couch to 5K group in Ballymacarbery, the closest village to where I live. I know a lot of them through being involved with the Neighbourhood Watch, and some text messages got sent to the wrong WhatsApp group, so I'm aware it's happening. Deedee has done a couple of marathons in Dublin, and she tells me that it has really helped her to cope with those dark experiences we share.

'Come on,' she tells me one evening when she drops over for a chat. 'Why not give it a go? What have you got to lose?'

I tell her not to be so daft. I'm in my forties and a smoker. Not in a million years is anyone going to turn me into a runner at this stage of my life.

'No one is saying you need to qualify for the Olympic team,' Deedee persists. 'It will help you physically and it has done wonders for my mental health.'

I sniff at that. How will dragging your arse up and down all the hills in the Nire Valley improve anyone's mental health? I would have thought that, if anything, ending up lying in a ditch wheezing like a clapped-out car would only make it worse!

'Running has really helped me to sleep,' Deedee says in a last-ditch attempt. 'After a good run, you're so shattered you're gone as soon as your head hits the pillow.'

I look up at that. My sleep patterns have become terrible, and I have the haggard, haunted look of an insomniac. I hate to admit it, but my mental state has been getting worse and worse every year that passes. You can only repress pain for so long without it finding a release. I've bottled my demons up for as long as I can, but I know something has to give.

'Really?'

'I promise. Just give it a go. Once. You'll be glad you did.'

Begrudgingly, I agree to attending one training session.

I arrive at the community centre the first Monday evening, and right away I think I've made a big mistake. Everyone in the group is at least half my age. I'm about to make an excuse and get out of there when the guy who is going to be training us, Colm Ryan, comes over and tells me how glad he is I'm there and, as if he's reading my mind, tells me to put all my doubts aside.

'You look like a runner,' he says.

I've always been tall and skinny, but I'd put it down to the years I did Irish dancing, backed by a fast metabolism.

'Well, I can assure you I'm not!' I shoot back at him.

'Not yet.' He laughs. 'But you will be.'

On the first night Colm brings us on a three-mile loop. To break us in gently, the session is structured in timed chunks: we walk for five minutes and then run for two. Colm is very rigorous and really encouraging, but by the end of it, I'm sure I'll keel over and never get back up again.

I had assumed it would be my chest and lungs that would be my biggest problems, but they are only a part of what feels like a complete physical assault. My legs are the first bits of me to complain – the backs of my calves become really tight, as if there is no flexibility in them at all. The small of my back starts to scream and every breath burns. I manage to get up the first hill, but by the time we are into the second mile, I'm certain I am going to have to stop. All around me, the group are in various stages of similar exhaustion, but I am only vaguely aware of their discomfort – all I care about is my own personal misery.

'I can't go on,' I wheeze at Colm, who is jogging happily along beside us, not so much as a bead of sweat on his brow, his breathing easy and unlaboured.

'You can slow down to a walk in one more minute,' he says airily.

'You don't get it: I'm finished!' I bark back.

'Not at all. Fifty seconds more, then you can walk.'

I mutter threats and obscenities under my breath, but for some reason I still don't understand, I keep going and make it back to the community centre with legs that feel like jelly and a chest that seems to contain two scorched and smouldering lungs.

'This is just not for me,' I tell Colm as he bids me goodnight.

'You'll be back.' He laughs.

'I really won't,' I say firmly.

'See you on Wednesday. I think you could have a talent for this.'

I shake my head in disbelief and make for the car park.

I sit in my car and stare at the steering wheel. Through the windscreen I can see all the other women heading off into the early evening, chatting to one another about what they've just done, and I realise that a part of me admires them. After all, they have just run and walked three miles of hilly, difficult road. While some have run before, for most it's the first time they've ever done something like this.

They have every reason to be proud of themselves.

And then it hits me: I have every reason to be proud of myself, too.

Wouldn't it be nice to have something, just for me, that I might actually be good at?

The next day, I buy my first pair of proper running shoes.

A Middle-Aged Woman Walks Into a Doctor's Surgery ...

My GP looks at me as if I've just gone mad.

'You've done what?'

'I've given up smoking and taken up running.'

He sits behind his old wooden desk, photos of his family smiling beatifically into the camera, a prescription pad at his right elbow. On the wall behind him is a poster of the food pyramid. I realise as I glance at it that my diet has gone to shite.

'Why?' he asks after a long pause.

He is one of the few people who knows about the abuse – I've had to tell him about it to explain my trouble sleeping and my depression. He is an understanding man, and I like him.

'I want to do something new, something that is all about me and no one else.'

He shakes his head and steeples his hands. He wears gold-framed glasses and they make him look quite old-fashioned, even though he's younger than me. 'You came to me more than a year ago because you weren't sleeping, and you were having intrusive thoughts.'

I nod.

'You're still losing weight. Eight pounds since you were last here.'

'Is that so bad?'

'Stephanie, you can't afford the loss. You're not carrying any excess.'

'Things have been difficult.'

He sighs and makes a note in my file. 'You are under a lot of stress. You know that I've been pushing you to kick the coffin nails for years, but I have to question if this is the best time to do it. Your blood pressure is through the roof. Do you really want to pile on another reason to be unhappy?'

'I'm hoping this will make me happier.'

He puts the pen down and looks me dead in the eye. 'Is it possible you're just finding new ways to punish yourself?'

'No. I want a challenge, something to get me outside of my head.'

He sighs deeply. 'All right. If you're determined to do this, I won't argue. Physical exercise can definitely help with depression, so who knows, maybe this is your psyche's way of helping itself. I'll renew your prescription for the sedatives, but you must eat properly and I want to see you again in a fortnight. If there are any detrimental effects from your new ... *regime* ... you should stop immediately.'

'I know.'

'You know where I am if you need me.'

'I'll see you in a fortnight.'

'Will I hum the music from *Chariots of Fire* as you leave?'

'If it makes you feel better.'

Body Popping

We are to run the Ballymacarbery 6K race towards the end of May, six weeks to the day from my first training session.

It dawns on me pretty quickly that, while I definitely want to run, I have never seen it as anything other than a private pursuit – the idea of running in front of people terrifies me. That spectators will know it's me, Stephanie Hickey, running in the open, surrounded by other athletes who are all, of course, going to be exponentially better than me, appals me.

I have a nightmare of my name being called out over a loudspeaker as I crawl on all fours across the finish line, having collapsed somewhere at the halfway point, every single person watching in fits of laughter at this ludicrous wrinkly old woman who has the misplaced belief she could ever be a runner.

I am afraid of looking stupid in my running gear.

I am convinced that I seem absurdly out of place among the other women from the Ballymacarbery group – like a granny they've taken out of the care home for the day.

I am certain that my running gait is all wrong and that I will be showing everyone up by participating.

I consider doing the run on another day, when nobody will be there to see me.

I articulate all this to Colm, our trainer, who in his quiet, firm way informs me that there is no way I am getting out of doing the run. 'It's an important part of the programme,' he says. 'It makes it official and completes this part of your training.'

I know what the problem is, but at this point I can't tell Colm. Other than Deedee (she and I rarely mention it), my GP and Angelo, I can't tell anyone.

The abuse makes even a simple activity like this difficult.

I have always had issues with my body. I am ashamed of it, disgusted by it. My physical self is something that I use to get around, but I have no love for it, and the thoughts of displaying my body, even covered up in spandex running gear, makes me feel a bit ill.

I also have a debilitating fear that it will let me down – that I'll throw up or need to use the bathroom or just fall down in a heap at the most inopportune time. I have never considered my body to be reliable or worthy. Over the years people have told me I am striking to look at, or that I seem strong or physically able, but I can never accept that. In my mind's eye, I'm ill-formed and ugly and sickly and useless.

The biggest obstacle for me as I train for this first race is overcoming this self-loathing. It is a hatred Bartholomew Prendergast instilled in me when I was a teenager, and it has never left me.

I go to the weekly training sessions, but I go out alone too in an effort to find mental pathways around the looming presence of Batty. As I battle the hills and laneways of the Nire Valley, I am also battling the shade of my tormentor. In those early days, as I turn out to train in the rain and the hail, the blistering sun or the blasting wind, his image is looming always over the horizon, peering down at me and leering, telling me I'm never going to make it.

But the sound of my brand-new professional running shoes drowns out his imprecations, and somehow, in spite of all my fears and worries, something happens I never expected – I start having fun.

I enjoy being with the other women. I've always been a bit solitary, a bit of a home bird. Suddenly I'm surrounded by a group of friends and confidantes, all with the same goal. My fears about my body become less pronounced because we're all pushing ourselves physically and (perhaps more importantly) we're all wearing unforgiving running gear and we're sweating and moaning and groaning and no one gives a damn.

And then there's Colm. He becomes my mentor, not just in the running, but emotionally too. And this is perhaps the biggest surprise for me in this new phase of my life.

I have learned through bitter experience not to trust men, that they always have an ulterior motive and are not to be taken into your circle of trust. Colm Ryan turns all that on its head. All he asks is that you show up and give your all. He listens to our bitching and complaining and whining and giving out with calm indulgence.

Knowing I am keen, he offers to come running with me outside the group sessions, and we sometimes work two or even three extra runs in during the week. I am now training almost every second day.

Sometimes it all gets too much and I sob uncontrollably as I run. He never bats an eyelid or asks what's going on – he just jogs stolidly and silently beside me, allowing the pain to be driven from inside me in an exorcism of physical exertion.

The Wednesday before the 6K I declare that there is no way under the sun I can complete the race, that I just don't have it in me.

'I'm terrified I won't finish it,' I tell Colm, the horror evident in my eyes.

'You're ready,' he says.

I don't believe him.

But I do the race anyway.

The Touraneena 6K
(or how I learned that
running might save my life)

The line of people chat quietly. A lot of them have come from other running clubs – Cork, Waterford and Dublin are represented – all here to do Touraneena's famous 6K loop. Some are checking their shoes; others are setting timings on their phones or Fitbits. A couple of very serious-looking guys are doing lunges at the back of the car park, expressions of grim determination on their faces.

And I'm dying for a cigarette.

Colm is giving the other women a pep talk, but I need

some space. I've barely slept over the past four nights, and all I can think right now is that I am not going to finish this without having to stop – I hope that I'll be able to at least keep walking if that happens, but I am fucking terrified that I'll actually collapse or throw up or get a dose of the shits.

Any and all of those things is possible because my stomach is doing cartwheels, and before I even begin my legs are shaking. Worst of all, my family have all come to see me finish. I made the mistake of telling my daughter, Danielle, about the race, and she is determined to be proud of me even if I can't be of myself. So she, Angelo, Philip, Dylan and Riccardo have gathered on the bridge, which is on the run-up to the finish, to cheer me in.

I wonder if they'll still be cheering so much if I'm Paddy last?

Of course they will. Even if I drag my sweat-soaked body over the line three hours after everyone else has gone home, my beautiful family will be there to give me encouragement. So why do I always feel I don't deserve their loyalty and love?

Colm calls to me that the race is about to begin.

The weather is perfect. It's a balmy May evening with a breeze light enough that it won't interfere with the run. We haven't had rain in a few days so the ground is dry, and on some of the hills we're going to be dealing with, that's a real benefit. All told, the conditions couldn't be better.

I follow the others to the starting line. Deedee is there in the pack, but she knows how nervous I am and she's leaving me to my thoughts. One of the other runners, a friendly girl called Siobhan, grins at me and gives me the thumbs-up. I try to smile back, but it probably looks as if I'm about to burst into tears.

We're actually lined up right outside the village graveyard, and I'm thinking to myself how appropriate that is when the klaxon goes off and we're away. I find that, despite all my worries, I've struck up a pace that is probably faster than I would usually go. Somehow instinct has kicked in and I feel good.

We go on through the village, and there is Danielle and the others, all calling my name and waving, and I have a moment where, despite everything, I think what a good-looking family I have, and then I'm past them and the village is behind me and we're on the roadway out towards my home place.

I put my head down and focus on the road, one foot in front of the other. The tarmac and the bits of gravel and scutch scroll past like through the window of a train. I feel my blood pumping and the air going in and out of my lungs and I am aware of the drag of another hill and so far so good. Maybe I can do this after all. Maybe I'm as good as Colm thinks I can be. Maybe I'm not a dead loss.

But it's too good to last. I hit the wall, that place in a run where the pain and the exertion gets too much and your body tells you that it needs to rest and where every grain of sense in you screams to *stop, stop stop*!

I look up and we're on the hill that leads to the main

Dungarvan road. For a second I marvel that I've actually made it so far, but then the pain comes like a tidal wave and I think I'm going to go down. From just behind me, someone says, 'My God, you set some pace, Stephanie!'

It's Siobhan, the girl I saw at the starting line. As I have slowed, she has caught up behind me.

'I'm struggling,' I manage to say, trying to smile at her again and still not succeeding.

'Join the club,' she pants, coming up beside me. 'You should go on ahead. We've all been commenting on how brilliantly you've done in the training. You're a natural.'

I marvel at what she's saying – have they really all noticed me? Have I stood out?

'Everyone reckons you're going to finish way ahead of the pack,' she continues. 'Have a breather with me and then take off. Show all these visitors how good we locals are.'

'Let's make a deal,' I say, my voice invested with a strength I wish I felt. 'Let's do it together.'

She nods and we both take off.

That hill nearly kills us both. By the time we are three-quarters of the way up it, Siobhan is flagging badly.

'I can't,' she says, her voice little more than a whisper.

'You can!' I urge her on. 'If you stop you won't start again. Look – there's the cross.'

We both haul ourselves over the brow, our bodies singing with the strain, and we're on the Dungarvan road.

'You know this is the halfway point,' I tell Siobhan.

'I never would have made it without you,' she says, laughing as we start down a gentle incline, our backs and calves humming with relief.

And I know I wouldn't have made it without her, either. By driving her on, I was also driving myself.

'Please, Stephanie, go on ahead,' she says moments later. 'I'm happy to plod along for a while.'

I feel as if I really could speed up, and I say to her, 'Are you sure?'

She nods.

'Just keep in mind that at the next crossroads, you're almost home,' I say as I hit the accelerator.

And now it's effortless. My muscles are moving easily and I'm in vernal heat and for the first time in more years than I want to remember I don't care about how I look or what people think of me and Batty sick-fuck Prendergast can go and rot somewhere. I am in the moment and it is beautiful. The trees never looked so gorgeous and the sky never seemed so blue and liquid and I am here in this place I love doing something I now understand God designed me to do.

After a time, I slow again so Siobhan can catch up – I want to share this and, for some reason, I want to share it with her.

We come back down into the village and I see that Colm has finished and is waiting for us on the bridge. The last stretch of the loop is a hill that seems almost vertical now, although I've walked it countless times.

'Eyes on the road, control your breathing and let's finish strong,' Colm says, falling in beside Siobhan and me.

I'd be lying if I said that last hill didn't hurt like all hell, but there is a photo of me crossing the finish line, an enormous grin on my face.

The Touraneena 6K was a special moment in my life. On the road I found something. I learned an important truth about life and about myself.

I learned I deserved to be happy.

All I had to do was make some changes.

In the Early Morning Rain

I get up at six and do my usual check-in to see that everyone in the house is all right.

I've started doing that, lately – I don't know why, maybe I'm a mother bear making sure that all my cubs are snug and secure. I peep in at bedroom doors and see tousled heads and hear regular breathing. Angelo, his dark Latin complexion rugged even in the early morning light, mutters something in Italian and rolls over for a last nap before he has to get up to go to the restaurant where he works.

I pull on my gear and have a quick cup of tea standing on the porch. There is a light drizzle this morning, but I don't mind. Sometimes the countryside around the Nire looks better through the prism of rainfall.

There is a lot going on in my life right now.

My father is ill – his health has been failing for years, and we all feel that he does not have long left. It is important to me that the time we have remaining is good, and that means there is unfinished business that needs to be concluded, things I have to do for him and for myself.

I take a deep breath and jog to the gate, then turn down the hill towards Ballymacarbery, then on to Newcastle. I'm planning on doing a long run this morning – I'll cover 12 miles before I see the gates of my home again.

At Rossmore, I double back and there is a road, set high on a bluff, that overlooks the wide countryside, Clonmel twinkling in the distance like a jewel. Up here the woods loom on my left and the trees are crowded with the whirr of wrens and the chatter of magpies and, somewhere in the canopy, the heckle of crossbills.

I know what I must do. I have known for years, but I have been reluctant to accept the hard truth of it.

I push my muscles up a gear and sense my inner circuit-breaker switching over. The endorphin rush hits me in a cascade of euphoria and in an instant I am filled with a sense of wellbeing and effortless physical grace. I am the wild countryside and it is me. My corporeal being is moving through the liquid sound of birdsong and the cool, sweet touch of the rain, and right now, I can do anything I set my mind to. Pain, unhappiness, feelings of unworthiness, all are blasted aside and I know that whatever comes, I can take it in my stride, for my stride is magnificent.

Tears come but they are not tears of sadness. I am gifted with the knowledge that this is my pain being siphoned from me by the spirit of the run. Somehow, the gods who govern this place and this pursuit are reaching out and taking my burden. I let them.

I know by the time I reach my front door again that I am going to the police that night.

I am going to press charges against my brother-in-law.

It has been thirty years coming.

I Know What You're Thinking

Let's get it out in the open now, shall we? I know exactly what you're all thinking, and I can promise you, there's nothing you can say that I haven't said to myself one hundred million times in the darkest hours of the night, when sleep seems a lifetime away.

Why, you're wondering, if the abuse started when I was twelve, did I wait until I was in my forties to do something about it?

And I can accept that it's a fair question. To answer it, we need to talk about what sexual abuse does to you.

One of the most powerful and insidious effects of child sexual abuse is the way it messes with your head. As I've already pointed out, I come from a loving, nurturing home where all I had ever experienced was positivity and affection. I was the apple of my father's eye, my mother raised me to be a strong woman and my siblings were protective and gentle with me.

Suddenly, with no warning, an adult I had been conditioned to trust and respect begins to act in a way that seems altogether strange and out of character. He hurts me. He forces me to do things I do not want to do, things every fibre of my being tell me are wrong and against the rules.

Surely, you're all saying to yourselves, Stephanie should have immediately gone to those caring, loving parents of hers and told them what had happened so they could deal with this wolf in sheep's clothing, this viper in their nest.

Would you believe me if I told you that such a thought did not even occur to me until months later, and when it did, I dismissed it right away? To be honest with you, and I am really trying to be honest here, once that first physical act was done, I tried to forget about it straight away. I pushed it far back into my head and did my best to pretend that it had all been an awful hallucination. Of course, it wasn't long before the disgusting letch was after me again, but still something in me froze and I just tried to get on with the other parts of my life and act as if nothing out of the ordinary was happening.

It's only in recent years that I've tried to understand this and question why I reacted the way I did. I can only write for myself and from my own point of view, but I have spoken to some other survivors, and it seems my reaction isn't that out of the ordinary.

But it is pretty damned complicated.

I don't want to dwell on this for too long, so I'm going to try and sum it up for you in five points, and then we'll get back to the story.

1. **I felt scared.** A man who, for all intents and purposes, I loved as a big brother had just forced me to do things that were alien and painful. He had ignored me when I had tried to say no, had used his greater size and strength to overpower me. And when it was all going on, he changed from the person I thought I knew into something monstrous – I was reminded of *Dr Jekyll and Mr Hyde*: it was as if something dark and rotten in him crawled out and the good person wasn't there any more. This was really frightening. All I wanted to do was bury the experience as deep as I could.

2. **I felt isolated.** He drove us to a place where he knew no one would see us. He hid the van behind a thicket of trees. When it was done, he told me it was our secret. I didn't understand what had happened, but I knew well enough that it was wrong and that this was something I shouldn't be doing. Somehow, by telling me it was just between us, he made me his accomplice, and that put me in a club with just me and him in it. He set me in opposition to my family. That was a place I'd never

been in before, and I remember a powerful sense of loneliness.

3. **I felt guilty.** I was a thirteen-year-old country girl growing up in the powerfully (and, let's be honest, slightly oppressive) Roman Catholic Ireland of the 1980s. I knew there was something called sex, and I had a vague sense of the mechanics of it, and I knew it was where babies came from, but other than that I was in the dark. What I very much thought I knew, though, was that outside of marriage and devoid of the purpose of creating children, sex was something dirty and shameful. Now here was Stephanie, allowing herself to be taken to a secluded spot on a rainy Friday night, and doesn't she get into the back of the fella's van and give him a blow job? We all know what kind of a girl does that, don't we? I was crippled with guilt. And shame.

4. **I believed I had betrayed my sister.** As soon as he'd had his fun, Batty drove us right to the house in Tallow. I had to sit across the kitchen table and look my sister in the eye while the taste of her husband was still in my mouth. All I could think was that she would be furious with me and that it would destroy the family if word ever got out. Try to remember that the Irish mindset at that time tended to place the blame for any kind of sexual indiscretion squarely on the shoulders of the women involved – the poor

men were seen as helpless pawns, slaves to their base drives, and we women were the temptresses, forever dangling forbidden fruit under their noses. I was convinced that I had done something to make this happen, that, unwittingly, I had repaid all of Tisha's kindness to me by cheating on her with her husband.

5. **I was sure no one would believe me.** Batty Prendergast was a hugely popular, well-known local figure. He fronted the most sought-after local band, he was a member of the golf club and he was friends with everyone. When the abuse began, he was about thirty years old, a man in his prime. I was barely even in my teens. Before he married my sister (and, I later discovered, long afterwards) he was known as something of a ladies' man, and he had the best-looking girls in the south-east of Ireland on his arm. Tisha had to do a bit of chasing to finally snare him. Why would anyone believe he would want anything to do with a scrawny, barely developed tomboy like me? It made no sense.

So you see, as bad as it was, I knew I had no power to stop what was happening, and my telling would turn my world upside down even more than it already was. And it bears repeating that I barely had the words to describe what had happened, never mind the wherewithal to know what to do about it.

I prayed someone would recognise the pain I was in and take even a little of it away. All I wanted was for someone to reach out, take my hand and say to me, 'I've got you, Stephanie. I've got you.'

But that never happened.

It seemed that the sensible thing to do was to stay quiet, put my head down and just try to get through it all.

And that's what I did.

Until I couldn't any more.

So Why Now?

What was it that made me decide to tell? There were so many factors. But I'll try to explain. I suppose I always knew I needed to tell, but I want to stress that it was a massively difficult decision.

I had gone over the pros and cons of going to the police countless times in my head, and the negatives always seemed to outweigh the positives. I worried about what it would do to Tisha and Batty's kids, and the impact on my parents and other siblings would be colossal.

I thought about how people would look at me: I knew that (in theory, at least) I could press charges anonymously, but this is a small community, and I was in no doubt someone would talk, and that someone would tell someone else, and before long everyone would know what had happened to me and what I had done. Batty was still a celebrated man, the life and soul of every party, and I was a no one – Tommy Hickey's daughter, the strange one who kept herself to herself.

I imagined all sorts of scenarios where I was refused service in shops and cafés, where my kids were bullied at school and where I lost what few friends I had. Angelo has always been patient and kind to me, but even his positivity has a limit – how could I ask him to put up with something as traumatic as this?

In the end, I had more or less decided that I would take this secret to my grave, but then Daddy became gravely ill. It started, as things like this tend to, slowly, and initially the symptoms looked just like the normal signs of old age. But gradually it became clear that the huge heart my wonderful father has always had was giving out. I scaled back my agency work so I could act as his carer (Mammy was beginning to exhibit the tell-tale traits of dementia, and there was no way she could do it on her own) and we all prepared ourselves for what we knew was coming.

One afternoon we were called to the hospital. Daddy had gone in a few days earlier, as he was having trouble catching his breath, but as we gathered in the Coronary Care Unit, it was clear the doctor was telling us to say our goodbyes, that we had perhaps a week, maybe a little more if we were lucky.

We took turns sitting with Daddy. He was drifting in and

out of consciousness – sometimes he knew I was there, sometimes he didn't, but all that mattered was that I could feel his hand in my own and that I could savour this closeness. I talked to him, telling him stories of when I was a small child and he would play the spoons and have me dance.

At some point I must have dozed off because I jolted into wakefulness and there, looming over my father's bed, reeking of cheap aftershave and orange Lucozade, was Batty Prendergast. His lower lip was trembling, and one of his greasy paws rested on my father's shoulder.

'He was the best man I knew,' my brother-in-law snivelled.

'Jesus, Batty, he's not dead yet!' I snapped.

'Tisha and I will take turns watching with you,' he said, his voice still heavy with tears. This surprised me, as Batty and Tisha had split several years ago when his womanising finally became too much for her. I was tempted to tell her, then, but when I saw the hurt his infidelity caused, I didn't want to add to it with my own sordid story. My sister now lives with another man, a part-time teacher in a nearby college. I am aware she speaks to Batty however, and he still has a huge influence over her life.

'There's no need,' I protested.

'It's decided,' he said firmly. 'You take a break now. I'll stay for the next couple of hours.'

I stood and fled the room.

Outside in the car park I took a cigarette from its pack with trembling hands (I had fallen back on the habit out of stress when my father became ill) and felt an anger such as I have never experienced. I had just been told I might have a week left with my father. I was damned if I was going to share it with the man who made my life miserable.

Daddy did his best, but he had never been able to rid us of this ogre in our midst. In recent years, I have come to believe my father was carrying a lot of guilt over what happened to me. A gentle-natured, sweet soul who always shied away from confrontation, Batty was too big a personality for him. There was always an edge when the two of them were together, always a sense that Daddy saw through his bluster, but my father was never capable of putting this unease into words and throwing the predator out of our house.

Now, when my father was at his lowest, I needed to be strong for him.

I would fight the monster myself.

Let Me Explain

Let me explain some things about the process I went through before I made the decision to go to the police because I want everyone reading this to know that it was not easy. It was probably the hardest thing I have ever done in my life.

And the reasoning behind it was complex.

In some ways, the decision was almost a reflex action. Knowing my father was dying and that he would, deep down, have wanted Batty to be brought to justice was a major factor. In some ways, my decision to press charges was about honouring my dad. I thought he would want to know, before he died, that I had fought back and beaten my abuser.

But that was only the start of it.

The thought of my abuser befouling the time I had left with my dad was also unbearable. My father's illness had brought Batty back into my life with jarring suddenness. I simply could not tolerate his proximity any longer.

I also knew, somewhere in the pit of my consciousness, that keeping the secret all these years was eating me up. The anguish, the self-loathing, the intrusive thoughts, were getting worse and worse. If I didn't do something soon to confront my demons, I was worried about what I might do to myself. And I had my partner and my children to think of. They needed me. Facing up to the truth of my past was the only way I could look them in the eye with a sense of pride and with my essence intact.

And, behind all of this, the running had given me a strength I didn't know I had. It gave me an escape, an identity and a support network I knew I could depend on. Taking to the road brought me peace and a calm centre. With that in place, I felt energised and empowered. Even if things got rocky and difficult, running gave me a safe place to go back to, an escape I could avail of at any time.

Angelo knew I was going to the police.

But I should probably talk a little bit about how I discussed this critical decision with the other members of my family.

Deedee had talked to me before about going to the police, but when she did I wasn't ready. Like the loving, thoughtful, selfless sister she is, she told me she would wait until I felt I was strong enough to face the trauma of pressing charges. I went to her house one evening shortly after Daddy had gone into hospital. It's funny: I knew exactly what I wanted to say, and had even mapped out our conversation in my head on the drive over, but when I got there, not a word would come. I sat in Deedee's living room with her and her husband (she and Ciaran were now married) a man I love like a brother, and I listened while they talked about the weather and local goings on, and all the while my head was awhirl.

I had made her wait so long. It had been me who had stalled, and now I had the gall to arrive at her home, demanding her life and that of her family be turned upside down simply because I had decided the moment was right for me. I felt selfish and cold-hearted and callous. As I sat there, hearing them laugh and joke about simple, joyous, uncomplicated things, I was sure I had made a terrible error. This was not the right time at all. It would never be the right time.

But, as usual, my wonderful sister came to my rescue.

'You don't look well,' she said after a while. 'Are you all right?'

I mumbled that I was fine.

'You said you wanted to tell me something.'

'It's nothing.'

She gave me a hard look, and something passed between us.

'It's about *him*, isn't it?'

There has only ever been one *him* for me and Deedee. I nodded.

'You're ready?'

I nodded again, trying not to let her see the tears in my eyes.

Ciaran grinned.

'We've talked about this, Deedee and me, and we knew you'd come around sooner or later,' he said. 'This is good. It's right.'

'It's going to be awful, though,' I said.

'Maybe,' Deedee said. 'But a lot of people have our backs. And the ones who don't, don't matter.'

Things didn't go quite so well with Mammy. Deedee and I talked to her the following day, and she tried to persuade us not to do it. I had thought she might be surprised or upset when I told her what Batty had done to me and my sister, but, never very demonstrative, she gave each of us a brisk hug, but then went straight to business.

'Your daddy is sick. This will only upset him.'

'Daddy wants us to press charges,' I said. 'I know he does.'

'How do you know? Have you asked him? Have you talked to him about what you're planning to do?'

As it happened, I had. I had spoken gently to my father about Batty just that morning. He had said very little – in truth, he was barely able to catch his breath to speak – but he had squeezed my hand and nodded his head when I asked for his blessing. It was enough.

Daddy would rally, defying the doctor's forecasts for his demise, and would live to see the end of this story. There were times when I know he found the going very hard, and on more than one occasion he told me he wished he could be spared the bad feelings the legal battle stirred up in all of us. But he also told me how proud he was of me.

And that meant more to me than anything else.

My mother, always the matriarch, asked each of us in turn to think about how this would devastate the family, the shame in front of our neighbours and friends and how difficult it would be for us, for our kids and partners.

'You need to think long and hard on this, Stephanie,' she told me gravely.

'I have, Mammy.'

She nodded.

'All right then. If this is what you want, I'll support you. Both of you.'

And she never went back on that promise.

Mammy needn't have worried about how my children would cope. As each of them had become old enough to understand, I had told them about what Batty Prendergast had done to me.

This might seem strange to someone who has never had to deal with familial sexual abuse, but for me it seemed absolutely essential that my children knew. After all, Batty Prendergast was still a very present member of our family.

I did my level best to ensure he was *never* alone with any of my kids, but I was also hyper-aware that I couldn't be everywhere at once. What if he called over when I was at work? What if Danielle went to check on my mother, as she often did, and he happened to be there? I wanted my sons and daughter to be fully aware of the kind of man he was so they would never be trapped by him like I was. If he knocked on the door and I wasn't there to protect them, they were to simply not open it. If they had no option but to grant him entry I had them briefed to make their excuses and get out at the first available opportunity.

And it wasn't just Batty Prendergast I warned them about. I know there are many other men like Batty out there, and indeed some women with those predilections too. My story became an object lesson for my kids: if it can happen to your mother, who was raised in a close and loving family, then it can happen to anyone. The only defence is to be vigilant and to speak out if you are made feel uncomfortable in any way at all – even by a look or a seemingly innocent touch.

So yes, I told my children as soon as I believed they could grasp the significance of what I was telling them. While I was convinced it was absolutely right to pass on this information, I was also conscious of the burden of it. I was in no doubt that hearing that their uncle had molested their mother had to be extremely difficult for them to process. And I also worried they would think less of me. My lack of self-esteem, my deeply rooted feelings that I was not entitled to love, even from my own offspring, caused me to fear that sharing this with Danielle and Philip and Dylan and Riccardo would ultimately destroy our relationships. As far as I was concerned, though, their safety was more important than any image they might have of me. I was prepared to lose some of their respect if that was what it took to protect them.

As I say those words, I realise how insulting they are to my incredible kids. Not for one single moment did any of them express – in words or actions – any lessening of their regard for me. All they ever did was support, nurture and love me. They stood by me through it all.

So as I prepared to make my statement, I told everyone I felt needed to know.

Everyone except Tisha.

The night before I went to the police, I rang Tisha and told her we needed to speak. I saw her daily in the hospital as we took turns watching Daddy, but this was not a conversation to have in such a public space. She said I should come over. Angelo drove me – he said this was not a visit I should make on my own. Tisha was sitting in her kitchen and I didn't pause for a beat – I knew I had to get this out before she had a chance to gather her breath, so I told her, plainly and as quickly as I could, what her husband had done to me and that I had decided, finally, to go to the police about it. During it all she stalked the room, bitter, hurt and angry.

'You need to be with your children now, Tisha,' I said when I was finished. 'They deserve to know what's coming and they need to be prepared for it. Take care of one another. Support each other through this.'

I was trying to look after her, doing my best to see she would be all right during what was going to be a very stressful and upsetting time for her.

Unfortunately, Tisha didn't want to hear me. I could see

she had gone to a place where she wasn't thinking rationally – all the shame and hurt and betrayal she had suffered over years of infidelity at the hands of Batty bubbled to the surface. Here was I, one of the women who, in her mind, had seduced her husband away from her. She could not contain her fury.

Angry words were spoken. I probably said some angry words in return. I wish I could remember what we said, but I can't. What stays with me is the fact that when I walked into that house, despite everything, Tisha was still my sister, but by the time I left, she was not. The awful things Batty had done to both of us became a wedge that finally drove us apart completely.

The pain was profound. I wanted to tell her I loved her, to say that I did not blame her for what had happened, that we were both victims, but seeing the hurt and the blame in her eyes directed at me, all my good intentions were blown aside.

As Tisha and I waged a verbal war on one another, Angelo, usually a quiet man and slow to anger, could not remain silent. He took me by the arm. 'I am taking you out of this house,' he said through clenched teeth.

'I'm sorry, Tisha,' I said. 'It's happening. Soon.'

'I hope you can live with yourself in the knowledge that you are ruining my children's lives,' she said as we departed.

I left in a flurry of tears. Angelo drove home in grim silence.

It was the last time I ever spoke to my sister.

More Than a Word

I give my statement to the police on 30 November 2015.

It is my son Riccardo's tenth birthday, and after I watch him cut the cake, I drive to Ballymacarbery to meet Garda David Mansfield, with whom I had made an appointment earlier that day. I had given him no indication over the phone as to the purpose of the meeting – I'd just said I wanted to talk to him.

I arrive at the local station at eight in the evening. I have no idea what to expect: like everyone, I have seen police shows on television, and I have a sense I will be in an interrogation room with a harsh light beating down on me while a rugged detective fires question after question at me until I break.

It isn't like that at all. David is a young man, clean cut and quietly spoken. When I arrive, he offers to make us tea, then sits me down in a pleasant and warm conference room and listens as I explain that I want to report an historic case of abuse, one that involves my brother-in-law – a well-known and well-liked local figure.

I admit that I have no idea where to begin, and he tells me to take my time. We have all night if necessary.

Beginning shortly after eight that evening, we finally stop at midnight, simply because I am too tired to continue, but we are still far from done. A police statement is a very detailed, thorough document (it has to be – this is the information that will be used to determine whether or not a crime has been committed and will dictate how it is prosecuted and investigated). The thing that bothers me more than anything else is that I have no accurate memory of specific dates and times that events occurred.

David tells me not to worry about that – we can check them all later. The most important thing, he says, is to get the story down.

I am amazed at how skilled an interviewer he is. He helps me to work out that certain events happened in summer and others in winter. He asks me about what songs were playing on the radio or the television, which of course help to date particular occurrences. He is incredibly patient with me and so sensitive. He repeatedly asks me if I would prefer a female police officer, but he makes me feel so safe and so understood that I am more than happy to go through this process with him.

I don't want to suggest this is a pleasant experience because it is deeply harrowing. When making a statement, particularly one regarding any kind of abuse (sexual, physical or emotional), you must go into the explicit detail. I relive many of my worst moments with David, and at times I have to excuse myself because I am physically sick. He waits patiently, a glass of water ready for me when I return.

I am also reminded that I am not doing this in isolation. There can be no doubt that my family will be affected, as I am asked to name each of them, explain where I fit in the Hickey chronology and talk about what they knew or didn't know. It is difficult and fills me with guilt.

It really hits me that this garda is the first person other than Deedee and Angelo to really hear the full extent of what I have been through. I cannot work out whether this is a good thing or a bad thing and decide it doesn't matter. It is what it is.

The other really monumental revelation happens about halfway through, as I describe the first time Batty forced me to have sexual intercourse with him.

'Can I stop you there?' David asks me apologetically.

'Of course,' I say, worrying I have upset him in some way.

'You came here this evening to report sexual abuse,' he says. 'What you are describing to me is rape.'

It is not an exaggeration to say my world fell apart at that moment. We have to break while David enters the details of this specific incident into the PULSE system (the garda computer network) and calls his bosses to inform them a rape is being reported and the assailant has been named.

But that is not what upsets me.

It is that a whole new layer of violation has been added to what I thought I had experienced. You might think 'rape' is just a word, but it isn't. It carries with it a world of obscene pain. I have lived my entire adult life believing I have been sexually abused and have almost reached a kind of accommodation with that. Now I have to reshape my concept of who I am and what has been done to me.

Bartholomew Prendergast raped me.

I go back to the station the following day and finish what I have started.

'I am going to need to speak to everyone you told about the abuse and the rape,' David explains as we finish the process. 'I can visit them or they can come in and chat to me here in the station – it's their choice *how* it's done, but it will definitely *need* to be done. This is a criminal investigation, so it's quite serious.'

That guilt hits me again – John is married now, and we hardly ever talk any more (I run into him in the shops, sometimes). Will he even remember conversations we had all those years ago? Could it cause him aggravation? What will his wife say about it? His children?

David reassures me. 'Stephanie, you don't need to worry about any of that. I can meet him on his own. No one else need know about it. And you are not to blame for any of this. You did nothing wrong. In fact, by coming forward, you have absolutely done something right.'

That makes me feel a little bit better.

When I have signed the document, attesting that I came to the station of my own free will, I call Deedee and Ciaran and tell them: 'It's done.'

Deedee is silent at the other end of the phone. 'There's no going back now,' she says at last, and I know she's right.

And I am actually glad. It seems that Batty has a reckoning coming.

A Long-Overdue Confrontation

The process of giving my statement brings other memories floating to the surface, too.

I begin to think about that meeting in the house in Tallow, and the story we had been told about Batty being sent to Father Crowley, and how that priest, a close friend of my family, had organised for my brother-in-law to see a psychiatrist.

The story we had all been led to believe was that Batty was 'fixed', yet he clearly hadn't been. My abuse had begun again as soon as I was asked to go back to Batty and Tisha's home, and his womanising had continued as well. Whatever had happened, Batty was in no way cured.

Deedee and I rack our brains trying to remember what

had happened back then, and I ask my mother about it, too. My father, who would have been the best source of information, is, of course, unable to share his recollections, but from what Deedee, Ciaran and my mother can remember, Batty had certainly gone to Clonmel for a few meetings (they suggest as many as four or five) and after that had gone to at least a couple of appointments elsewhere – we assume with a psychiatrist or doctor of some kind – although he never divulged which mental health professional it was or even what the explicit purpose of those appointments were.

This begins to bother me a lot.

I have long accepted the distinct possibility my parents had not known at the meeting that Batty had abused me, although it seems now that they had come to suspect at a later date that he had. Yet still, with all the knowledge they did have – knowing about his abuse of my friend – how had they felt it was OK to send me back into such a dangerous environment? What assurances had they been given that he was 'cured'?

I try to ask Mammy about all of this, but her response is always the same: she can't remember, it was all so long ago, and it had been Daddy who had dealt with all of it.

'What do you want to be dragging all this up for?' she asks me. 'No good can come of it, surely? If you have to go to the police, fair enough, but why don't you just let them do their job?'

But that is something I struggle with. Back when that

meeting happened I was a child and I sat back and allowed other people to make decisions that deeply impacted on my life. Now I am an adult, and I will not remain silent.

I want answers.

Finally, I make the decision to go and speak to Father Crowley myself.

The priest is now in his mid-seventies, but he is still active in the community and a well-known face. I arrive at his door one afternoon, and as he brings me into his sitting room I do not beat around the bush.

'I need answers,' I tell him. 'And it seems that you're the only person who can give them to me.'

I do not even have to tell him what it is I'm talking about. I see it in his body language and can hear it in the tone of his voice. He seems very ill-at-ease, he shrugs a lot and looks at his feet. This is a hundred miles away from the confident, upright priest I have known my whole life. I remind him that he is almost a member of my family – that my parents always treated him as a surrogate son, that our door was always open to him and that clearly, in this instance, my father had put his trust in him to see that something was done about a problem that was putting not just me, but other young people in the community at risk.

'Well, they came to me here,' he begins.

'Who did?' I shoot back. 'Batty and Tisha?'

'Yes. They came to see me one evening many years ago.'

'What did they want?'

'They said they had problems. Problems in their marriage.'

'And did they specify what these problems were?'

'No. I referred them on. To someone I believed could help.'

I am trying not to get angry, at this point. It is clear to me that Father Crowley, a man I have considered a friend for as long as I can remember, is being decidedly reticent in how much he is prepared to tell me. It makes me feel like that child sitting outside the meeting all over again, waiting for the grown-ups to sort everything out. I am, of course, aware that confidentiality may be an issue, but it seems to me that my direct involvement in the case should in some way supersede that. Father Crowley obviously doesn't agree.

'Who did you refer them to, Father?' I ask.

He takes a deep breath and for a moment I think he may actually give me a straight answer. He doesn't.

'It doesn't matter now. He's dead.'

I try to keep the anger from my voice, but I'm not successful.

'It matters to me! I think I have a right to know.'

He is gazing at his shoes as if they might tell him how to get this annoying, angry woman out of his living room. When his footwear fails to offer him any means of escape, he looks up at me, and says, 'I sent your brother-in-law to a psychiatrist. Someone I thought could help him.'

I shake my head in exasperation.

'Father, you are asking me to believe that a young couple come to you, claiming they have some sort of marital problems – which you decide not to ask them to explain in any way – and your first thought is to send one of them (not both) to a psychiatrist? I have to tell you, I find that very hard to understand. Problems could have meant difficulty conceiving or managing their money or they could have been losing their faith.' I went on. 'Why not call a medical doctor or an accountant? Why was your first thought a psychiatrist?'

He takes a long, deep breath and says, 'I've already given a statement to the police.'

And there it was.

'Then you know how important this is to me. The bottom line is, Father, I was told you sent Batty Prendergast to someone to be fixed, but my abuse continued. I want to know who fixed him. I'd like a name, please. So I can go and annoy them instead of you.'

'I gave the police the name of the psychiatrist. They know everything.'

'Father, I'm sitting right here in front of you. Why can't you tell me?'

He looks as if he is about to bolt from the room for a moment, and then he finally says, 'His name was Morrison. Your sister and her husband told me he was having what they called "women problems". Dr Morrison specialises in matters of a ... a sexual nature. I thought he might be able to offer some advice. He died last February.'

I know I am being fobbed off, but I keep pushing.

'I don't care that he's dead. Who did he work for? They must have files, records...'

'All of which would be sealed and confidential.'

'Not in a case like this. There are child protection concerns. Did Dr Morrison work for the HSE? Was he a private consultant?'

'I think he was attached to the hospital.'

'Father, I'm going to look up this doctor, and I am going to go and ask the people he worked for about this whole business. But I may be back. Don't think this is over.'

The fact that I am leaving seems to give him some of his confidence back.

'Stephanie, I know you're angry now,' he says as he follows me to the door. 'But I want you to know that I'm praying for you.'

I stop and look him dead in the eye.

I tell him, 'Maybe you should save your prayers for someone who needs them.'

And I leave him standing there.

I drive down the road a little way and pull over. On my phone I do a web search for Dr Morrison. It doesn't take long to find out that he was, indeed, a psychiatrist, and he was attached to a hospital in Tipperary. I'm beginning to think that maybe Father Crowley had been more truthful than I'd given him credit for, when I come to the final line in Dr Morrison's biography – he was originally from Tallow, County Waterford.

My heart sinks. To me, it feels as if the old boys network has closed ranks to protect one of their own.

Now I need to add here that this is purely what it felt like. It is possible that Dr Morrison did his best and Batty ran rings around him and played along so it looked as if he was cured. I also feel I should point out that Father Crowley did nothing legally wrong according to the laws of the time – there were no clearly defined procedures for reporting child sexual abuse in the 1980s. The priest acted as well as could be expected. Even if he did report Batty to the police back then, there is no reason to believe the gardai of the 1980s would have even acted on the information.

All of this is true, and I can acknowledge it intellectually.

But it doesn't take away from the fact that I was let down. I was failed. I was left in a situation where I was being repeatedly abused and no one, it seems, can give me a reasonable explanation of why it happened.

I later learn that Dr Morrison saw Batty privately, in his own home, and no records for the meetings have been retained, if there ever were any. This feels like the final slap in the face. These appointments were not set up through the correct channels – the HSE and the hospital knew nothing about them.

Father Crowley maintains he knew nothing about Batty being a child sex abuser.

There is nothing I can do now but believe him.

However that makes me feel.

CENTRAL CRIMINAL COURT, DUBLIN

AUGUST 2018

How Can You Sum Up
So Much Pain?

When the final victim impact statement is read, all eyes turn to Justice Creedon.

'I have just listened to very compelling and deeply unsettling victim impact statements,' she begins. 'The scope and detail of the emotional damage experienced by these women is clear to me, and I want to assure all here present that I will give every single facet of information due consideration.'

What does this mean? Will court be adjourned for a couple of hours? Will we come back again after dinner?

'I also want to underscore the gravity of the case,' Justice Creedon continues. 'One of the victims was nine years old at the time the molestation began, and in all three cases there was repeated and habitual interference over extended time periods. I see clear signs of premeditation and the most cynical grooming.'

These words do my heart good: there can be no doubt we have been heard. This judge understands. It is a deeply significant moment for me.

'With all of this before me, I do not, in all good conscience, believe I can or should pass sentence today. I need time to think very carefully about everything that has been revealed.'

Now there is uproar. One of Batty's legal team jumps up and shouts over the hubbub. 'If it pleases, Judge, we would very much like to have a number of character references read into the record on behalf of Mr Prendergast! With the greatest of respect for the court, we have only been privy to one side of the man he is, and these documents can only aid you in your deliberations.'

The judge bangs her gavel and there is silence. 'I do not think I am inclined to hear the testimonials,' she says, looking down at the barrister. 'I have no doubt your client has done many works of corporeal duty over countless decades in his locality. There are several ways of looking at what the motivation behind such acts may have been, but for now, I will not test the goodwill of the families he has hurt by forcing them to sit through a celebration of his finer points. You may submit the documents and I will take them under advisement.'

'But, Judge, can I just say—?'

'My decision has been made.'

'Judge, Mister Prendergast is held in the highest of esteem by many community leaders in west Waterford. His work for the elderly in Dungarvan and Clonmel has been particularly celebrated, and despite some of the comments that have been made this afternoon, he has been a model father – his children have nothing but praise for him. Is it not indicative that, in the face of the most abhorrent of allegations, his entire family remain at his side?'

'Allegations he has pleaded guilty to,' Justice Creedon says. 'And I would hardly say his whole family are offering support when two of them have given the most damning evidence against him.'

'My client plays music for adults with special needs free of charge—'

I am upset now. How can anyone defend Batty after what he has done?

The barrister sits down and the judge is writing furiously on a legal pad. We all wait. There is nothing else to do. Finally, she sits upright and straightens her black robes.

'I am going to adjourn for sentencing until 26 November,' she says.

Three months. I am going to have to wait three months. I put my head in my hands.

Batty's barrister is up again. 'If it pleases the judge, my client would like to offer that he go to prison immediately. He believes that this would be the least stressful option for his immediate and ... extended family. As Stephanie Hickey and Deirdre Fahey have made the decision to waive anonymity, he feels it would be the kindest option.'

Justice Creedon writes something else down. 'Might I inform your client that this is not his decision to make? That said, he will be going down today. Court is adjourned.'

We hug and cry and tell each other we have done it – Batty is going to jail.

For exactly how long will remain unknown for some time to come.

WEST WATERFORD

2016

Fear of the Dark

I like to run in the daylight – I rarely run at night, and when I do, I must have someone with me. My favourite time is early in the morning when the day is fresh and bright, scrubbed clean by the dew and beaming with newly minted sunshine. Everything is resplendent and sparkling and I feel as if I am the first person to see all this beauty, and even on my worst days it gives me a sense of wellbeing.

The darkness is full of rumour and slithering, crawling things just beyond the limits of my vision. The gift running gives you is a sense of clarity, and in the sunshine I can see every bead of rain clinging to each branch, even high up in the trees. In the darkness I fancy I can make out lurking hunched figures cowering in the ditches waiting to spring out at me, their powerful limbs capable of bursts of speed I could never hope to summon.

When I was a young child, the dark held no such horrors. I could wander from room to room in the schoolhouse in the hours of winter darkness without ever needing to switch on a light – I knew every hallway and every stair by touch, and the house held no fear for me, as it was a place of love and light, regardless of the time of day or night.

Fear did not enter my life until *he* did.

My night-terrors are another of Batty Prendergast's gifts.

I have read that some children who have survived sexual abuse will, if asked to draw their bedrooms, sketch a picture in which the stick figure representing themselves will be shown sleeping *under* the bed rather than on top of it, a pathetic attempt to hide from the heinous things that so often visit them in the darkest hours of the night.

This is something I understand all too well. Ever since the abuse I have been afflicted with crippling insomnia, and I know its origins are those nights I spent in Tallow, knowing the bedroom door could be pushed open at any moment and I would be summoned to my brother-in-law's foul services.

Eventually, I would not bother to go to sleep at all and would lie awake, earphones in place, Dionne Warwick's soothing voice a kind of waking anaesthetic, and wait for his arrival. Night in Tallow was a time of evil.

Now, as an adult, I sometimes rise when it is still dark. I put on my armour – several layers of Lycra and my best running shoes – and I set off while the moon is still riding atop the clouds. I begin the climb into the Comeraghs as the sun is tipping its head above the horizon line, and as each beam of light erupts into the sky, I cry aloud and push onwards, higher, higher, until finally, in an explosion of radiance, night is banished and I am running directly into the path of a new day.

Light has won. Darkness is no more.

But that life were so simple.

The Accidental Runner

My nephew Quentin is home from Australia and I am thrilled to see him. He and I have always been very close, as we are about the same age, and right now, with the statement being made and the impact it has had on my relationship with Tisha, I need all the friends I can gather around me.

Independently of me, he has become interested in running and fitness in Oz and has done several triathlons since I saw him last, and he promises to do a run with me now he is back home.

I see there is a 5K taking place in nearby Dungarvan the first Sunday of his visit, and I book places for us both.

I call over to the former schoolhouse on the Saturday

to discover a session in full swing: everyone is enjoying a drink and songs are being sung. Quentin grins up at me and asks what my poison is.

'I will not be imbibing this evening, and neither should you be,' I scold him. 'Have you forgotten that we're both running tomorrow?'

Since my success in the 6K, I've been living a very virtuous existence, getting up early to run, going to work, eating healthily, often running a second time in the evenings and avoiding alcohol. The thoughts of drinking even a few glasses of wine on the day before a race seems tantamount to heresy.

'Sure, we're not running until four o'clock tomorrow afternoon,' Quentin says, his voice already slightly slurred from his merrymaking. 'Why not have one or two? We haven't had a family get-together in ages!'

I agree to stay for just one.

I think I got to bed around three o'clock on Sunday morning.

Neither Quentin nor I are feeling much like athletes by the time the following afternoon's race rolls around, but I am determined we will participate, hangovers and all. We arrive at the West Waterford Athletics Club in Dungarvan in good time, and I go to the desk to sign in and collect our numbers.

'Could you just run through the route for me?' I ask the steward, and he produces a map and begins to sketch out exactly where the race will take us.

'That doesn't sound like 5K,' I say warily.

'That's because it's not,' my host responds matter-of-factly. 'You've signed up for the five-mile race.'

To be clear, five miles translates to just over eight kilometres – a lot more than I was expecting. Add to this the fact that I've had very little sleep and am sporting the worst hangover I've had in years, and the whole project suddenly seems a bit more challenging than I had anticipated. Quentin cannot stifle a guffaw.

'What the hell have we gotten ourselves into?' I ask, my head throbbing rhythmically.

'We'll be grand,' Quentin says, taking down half a bottle of water in a single gulp. 'It'll help us to sweat all this booze out.'

'You needn't go galloping off like a greyhound,' I warn him. 'I'll need to take a very handy pace or I'll never manage.'

Quentin agrees, and we set off.

I have never been fixated on the times I achieve when I run – it just doesn't interest me, to be honest. A lot of very serious runners will ask you about your 'splits', which is a term used to describe how long it takes you to cover a specific distance (for example in this five-mile race, people asked me afterwards what my 'mile split' was, and I hadn't a notion). For me, it's always been about the pleasure of the experience itself – how long it takes to do it seems a bit pointless.

If other people get something from knowing, then more

power to them. It's just never been a consideration for me.

We complete the race, and to my surprise, I really enjoy it. Running with Quentin, whom I love dearly, is great fun, and we both cross the finish line with huge smiles on our faces and (suddenly starving) go to have some post-race refreshments in the athletics club.

While we are there, my friend Maria, who has done marathons and races all over the world, comes over to congratulate me. 'My gosh, Stephanie, you achieved a really great time in that one!'

'I had a good race, but I hardly think it was one of my best runs.' I laugh and tell her about last night's fun.

As I tell the story, I notice she is with a man – I don't know him at all – who listens in amazement as I recount our comedy of errors. She introduces him as Eamonn Cashin and tells me he is her trainer, which is not unusual: runners as dedicated as Maria will often have personal trainers who tailor programmes specifically for them and their unique needs.

The two of them join us for tea and sandwiches, and Eamonn seems truly amazed that I have performed so well in the race after a night of hard carousing.

'You didn't get to bed until 3 a.m.?' he asks me again a little while later.

'Nope.'

'And you were *drinking*?'

'Drinking might be too gentle a word for it,' I admit ruefully.

He pauses, consulting a notebook. 'But there's no disputing it – I timed you myself. How did you run so well under those conditions?'

I shrug, embarrassed now. 'I just did what I always do,' I say. 'I put one foot in front of the other until the race was done.'

'I've been a trainer for a long time,' he says, 'and I have to tell you, I think you're something special. To have done what I just saw you do – you must have extraordinary inner strength.'

'Not at all! I run because I enjoy it,' I say and leave it at that.

He looks at me for what seems a long time without saying anything and then changes the subject.

As Quentin and I are walking back to the car, my nephew says to me, 'I know Eamonn. I was in the class behind him in school.'

I throw him a look. 'So what?'

'He's the real deal. If he says you've got something special, then he's probably right.'

I laugh it off, telling him to stop messing, and we drive home.

The following day at work I get a text message. Eamonn has gotten my number from Maria, and he says he'd like to train me. His text includes information about a half-marathon taking place in Waterford in January, and Eamonn reckons I could do really well in it.

I don't respond to this text. I am full of mixed emotions. It is so long since anyone has seen anything positive in me, I'm not sure how to cope with it.

Later that evening, over dinner, I ask Angelo and in his beautiful, simple way he cuts straight through all my confusion. 'Do you want to do a half-marathon?' he asks.

'I'd fucking love to do one,' I answer without a pause.

'Then text the man back and say yes,' he retorts, deadpan.

And that is how I, a middle-aged woman who had been running for three months, acquired a qualified, experienced personal trainer and found herself running in the Viking, one of the most celebrated half-marathons in Ireland.

It seems it was a good idea to have those drinks after all!

A New Regime

Imeet Eamonn Cashin for a coffee a week after the five-mile race in Dungarvan. I am a bundle of nerves and still think he is possibly making fun of me. I've been doing my research, and I now know that:

1. A half-marathon is 13.1 miles, which translates to 21.08 kilometres – more than *four times* what I am used to running.

2. It is suggested that you should rack up *at least* forty miles a week if you are training for a full marathon, meaning twenty would be necessary for a half-marathon. I'm not coming anywhere close to that and wonder where I'll find the time.

3.   Every single marathon-related website I look at has paragraph after paragraph about the dangers of *chafing* – a kind of severe burn caused by your sports clothes repeatedly rubbing against your skin. Imagine carpet burn but without ever lying down. What kind of idiot participates in an activity so ridiculous your clothes turn against you? I sit at my computer, my mouth hanging open, gawping at photos of people with bloodstains over their nipples. Not good!

4.   Running marathons has a detrimental effect on your immune system. While moderate, regular training helps you fight off diseases, doing too much will actually cause you to become run down. Many runners report heavy bouts of the flu and colds in the weeks after running serious-distance races. Why would I want to make myself sick?

5.   Your toenails will possibly turn black and fall off. Many long-distance runners see this as a rite of passage. It sounds horrible and a bit frightening to me.

What it all boils down to is that human beings are not designed to do this kind of activity!

But despite all of these good reasons not to do the race, I still want to.

When I meet Eamonn, one of the first things I do is tell him that, whatever programme he puts in place for me, my Monday- and Wednesday-night runs with Colm and the girls from Touraneena are sacred, and he will just have to work them in somehow. Those runs have become a really important part of my week, and I look forward to them. Anything that might get in the way of those is immediately off the table. Eamonn promises he can devise a regimen that incorporates running with my friends and addresses the longer endurance training on other days.

As soon as he agrees this, my doubts melt away, and shaking his hand, I tell him I'm in. Grinning, Eamonn pulls a sheet of paper out of his bag and begins to spell out the plan.

I will begin by doing five miles. This seems doable, as I've already done a race of this distance, and it didn't faze me at all.

'You'll do two days of five-mile runs, and we'll work in different terrains – one flat, one a little more hilly and challenging. Then you take a day off.'

I nod in agreement, not telling him I actually find running on the hills easier.

'Then we push it up to seven miles. Two days of that.'

In the space of a couple of weeks, Eamonn will have me running twelve-mile routes. He assures me this is enough to prepare for a half-marathon. I'll have to take him at his word. I had assumed I'd be doing fifteen miles to make sure I was physically capable of the thirteen and a bit, but with grave seriousness, my new trainer informs me that this is generally considered to be over-training. Part of the race experience is the adrenaline, which pumps you full of endorphins (the body's naturally occurring painkillers) and pushes you to go a bit further and a bit harder than you normally would.

So my new training regime begins.

As well as my two short evening sessions with my friends, I now get up most days at six and do my long training runs. Eamonn and I work out different routes, many of which mirror parts of the Viking half-marathon course.

And as the distance I am covering grows longer and I chalk up those miles, something remarkable, almost miraculous happens: I look in the mirror and I take pleasure in what I see looking back at me. I feel good about my body, proud about what it can do. For the first time in many, many years, when I think about who Stephanie Hickey is, I don't think: *I'm Stephanie Hickey, the little girl who was sexually abused by her brother-in-law*; instead I think: *I'm Stephanie Hickey, and I'm a runner!*

And that is a powerful thing to be. A good thing.

Running has given me back my identity.

Learning Who Your Friends Are

In the days, weeks and months after I give my statement, David Mansfield makes sure I am fully involved in the process that immediately clicks into action.

He introduces me to Clare, who is to be my liaison – it is her job to ensure I fully understand each and every step of the procedures that are now happening all around me. This makes life a lot easier: I am naturally nervous about everything, and to her credit she calls me almost every day and explains what has occurred since we last spoke – 'David interviewed such-and-such a person yesterday evening and they gave us some very important information' or 'We're almost ready to send the file to the Director of

Public Prosecutions. It'll be up to her to decide whether or not there is enough evidence to take to court.'

That last bit of news causes me to get very jumpy indeed – I had thought that, once I decided to press charges, court would follow automatically. That, after all this fuss, someone who has never even met me can still decide the whole thing might be unworthy of a trial is mind-boggling to me.

'It's a formality,' Clare reassures me. 'I promise you, there is more than enough evidence to make them sit up and take notice.'

'You're sure?'

'Nothing is certain, Stephanie,' Clare says. 'But based on my experience, which is not inconsiderable, I'd start packing for Dublin if I were you.'

Here was another bolt out of the blue.

'Dublin? I thought the case would be heard in Waterford!'

In every imagined scenario, I have seen myself and Deedee in the courthouse in Dungarvan.

'Charges of this gravity are never heard in the Circuit Court,' Clare explains patiently. 'Your case will go straight to the Central Criminal Court.'

I don't know whether to laugh or cry.

'I know it's scary, but this is actually really good,' Clare continues. 'It's a sign of how seriously you are being taken.'

I have something I need to share with Clare. She has been at pains to tell me that the entire case can be heard *in camera*, which means in secret and without the media being allowed access.

Deedee and I, however, have decided to waive our anonymity.

We are going public.

David and Clare sit down with me and my beloved sister and spend a couple of hours talking about what this decision will mean.

The media will be permitted into the courtroom – we will appear on television, on radio, in newspapers and magazines. Everyone will know what we have been through, and reporters and editors will put their own spin on the details, playing up certain aspects of the story in ways we might find upsetting.

'Once there is a verdict, they can say what they like,' Clare advises us. 'It's unlikely, because of the nature of the case, but there could be some crazy journalist out there who decides to come down on Batty's side. They could write really nasty things about you. Are you prepared for that?'

'The important thing,' I tell them, 'is that Batty Prendergast is named. This is my gift to him – that he will never be able to hide who and what he is any more. They can say what they like about me. I want it known what this scumbag did. To me and to Deedee and to anyone else he interfered with.'

'Your family are already upset with you.' David tries another approach. 'By allowing yourselves to be named, you are permitting them to be identified too. You are waiving *their* anonymity.'

'You told me on the first evening I came in here that I have done nothing wrong,' I say. 'I have no reason to be ashamed, so why should they feel bad about being associated with me?'

'You're right, of course,' David says, smiling sadly. 'But unfortunately, the world isn't that simple, and people can be very cruel and small-minded.'

'This is how it often works,' Clare explains. 'The community divides into two camps: those who believe and support you, and those who stand by Batty.'

'You are going to learn who your true friends are,' David says. 'I hope you're ready.'

In the days, weeks and months that follow, I will receive messages of support from the most unexpected places. People I have never met before will walk up to me in the supermarket to tell me what my courage has meant to them. Women will contact me on social media and tell me their stories, some of which make mine look mild in comparison. Men I don't know will be at pains to tell me how ashamed they are that someone like Batty Prendergast is even included as a member of their gender group. Friends of my children will send me text messages of love, friendship and solidarity.

But there is always the other side of the coin.

I will be mocked, belittled, accused of dishonesty and subterfuge by people I thought I could trust. It will be suggested that I am money-grabbing (this makes no sense, as there is never payment involved), attention-seeking and morally repugnant. I will be berated for ruining the life of a 'good man' and told that I brought it all on myself and that I knew exactly what I was doing – that *I* took advantage of *him*. Some women will look at me as if I am scum, and some men as if I am easy.

And I don't care.

I know the truth.

And it set me free.

#MeToo

In Ireland, survivors of sexual abuse have the right to privacy under the law. This is right and proper because, as I think you have probably already gathered from spending some time with me, shame and guilt are a huge part of the legacy of being abused. Survivors *should* be able to press charges without having the whole world know what they have been through. The same thing extends to their families.

The fallout from rape and sexual abuse can be vast: there are all sorts of psychiatric problems, mood disorders, sexual dysfunctions, body dysmorphia, domestic violence, addiction issues and a litany of other difficulties that result from the attentions of a predator, and the families of victims have often been through a hell of a lot before a court case is even on the cards.

Another factor is that the vast majority of cases (and I mean the *vast* majority, as much as 80 per cent depending on which studies you read) are historic, dealing with abuse that occurred upwards of twenty years ago. This means that the investigations can be long and there are extended periods of stress and anguish, during which time no one knows if enough evidence is going to be gathered to even make a case worth pursuing.

The last thing a stressed family needs is to have reporters and cameras camped outside their door as the media comes looking for a story.

So right from the off, let me state that I think anonymity is an essential part of the legal process when it comes to the prosecution of sex offenders.

The downside of this, however, is that to protect the identities of the survivors, the identities of the offenders have to be kept a secret too. Think about it: in a country as small as Ireland, most people could very easily put two and two together and work out who the victim is once they know the name of an abuser.

So the privilege of anonymity is a double-edged sword: by protecting the victim it also stops the general public from knowing who the offenders are in their midst.

Deedee and I were very clear that, while neither of us relished the idea of the whole world knowing about the sordid business, we were damned if we would protect

Bartholomew Prendergast from the spotlight. Being the very public, ego-driven man that he is, we knew the greatest punishment for him would be for everyone to know who and what he is.

We also wanted to send a message to other young boys and girls who have been through the hell we had and who had a fear of coming forward. It was critical to us that they saw two women, frightened and battered by the whole experience, but coming out the other end of it nonetheless.

There has been a lot in the media recently about victims of sexual assault banding together and saying *no more*! All kinds of women, particularly in the film industry and the media, have stood up and talked about their experiences at the hands of powerful men, how they were manipulated and pressured into doing things they didn't want to do.

I applaud them for doing that, but my message is a little different.

Sexual molestation in all its forms exists everywhere. It's been with us since human beings lived in caves, and I believe it'll be with us long into the future. It isn't just women who are victim to it, either. Women, children and some men find themselves falling victim to individuals with too much power, people who believe they can do whatever the hell they want with complete impunity.

In Ireland we have had story after story coming out about abuse within organisations run by the church and other institutions. The UK saw similar horror stories coming from various radio and TV channels, where presenters and DJs acted like animals with children and young women.

The thing all these stories have in common is power: people in positions of power feel they can behave in the most abominable ways. By bestowing such power we are creating monsters. I believe the only way to put a stop to this kind of abuse is to stop creating figures who are so idolised. Priests, community leaders, showbiz personalities – they are, at the end of the day, just people and are therefore victim to human weakness. With such weakness can come corruption. The first step to fighting it is to acknowledge it as a possibility.

In our lives, Batty Prendergast was a powerful figure. He did whatever he felt like doing and nobody questioned him about it.

By waiving our anonymity, Deedee and I took our power back, and that is why we did it. We stood up, we owned our truth and we faced him down. It was difficult and it was painful, but by God it was worth it.

I do need to say here, however, that not everyone in our family agreed with us.

That's another gift my brother-in-law left us: he drove a wedge right down the middle of my wonderful, close-knit family.

With the precision of a surgeon, Batty Prendergast tore the Hickeys apart.

And that is something we have not been able to take back.

The Complicated
Process of Arrest

'So when are you going to arrest him?' I ask David Mansfield.

We are sitting in my kitchen drinking tea. Angelo is at work and Riccardo is at school and it feels as if years have passed since I gave my statement (in reality it has been a month). Batty is still wandering about as if he owns the world, playing golf, doing gigs in pubs, and it is driving me a little mad.

Add to this the fact that everyone else in the family (everyone except Batty, that is, who must know it's coming but seems utterly oblivious according to those family members who are in contact with him) is on tenterhooks waiting for it all to kick off and you will understand why I am a bundle of nerves.

'Soon,' David reassures me. 'It will happen very soon.'

'Can you not tell me when?' I press him.

'You know I can't do that.'

'Why, for the love of God?'

He explains it to me again.

An arrest is a complicated thing, usually involving a team of uniformed gardaí and detectives. Arrests tend to be done early in the day (there are rules about how long a person can be questioned and held before being formally charged, so the earlier an arrest occurs, the better) and the police will try to establish the person's movements and routines beforehand, so they will know where they are likely to be (you can't arrest someone if they're not physically present).

'If I tell you we are going to pick up Batty next Monday morning—'

'Are you?'

'No. But say I told you that.'

'So this is hypothetical?'

'Yes. I give you that time, and you promise not to tell anyone.'

'I wouldn't tell a soul.'

'You say that, but maybe you'd let something slip to Angelo. Or Danielle.'

'I never would.'

'Yeah, but you might. They know you really well, and maybe they pick something up from a hint you dropped or you write something down and they see it. Or one of them is outside the door when I tell you and they overhear. Do you get what I'm saying?'

'I suppose so ...'

'So Danielle might know. And she's very close to your mother. And without realising it, she lets something slip to her—'

'And somehow it gets back to Batty.' I finish the train of thought for him.

'Exactly. So we are all geared up to arrest Mr Prendergast. We have the men in place, the interview room prepped, the electric blanket turned on in the cell in the police station all ready for his arrival, and we swoop in for the arrest, only for one important point.'

'He's not there.'

'Our boy has decided on the spur of the moment to take part in a golf tournament in Leitrim. Everything is put on hold. You're pissed off, I'm upset, my boss is furious – can you see why we keep this on a need-to-know basis?'

I have to agree with David. There are some things you are better off not knowing.

Batty is arrested at 6.30 a.m. on a Monday morning as he arrives to his place of work. There is quite a crowd of onlookers. It must be very humiliating.

Rather than going to Dungarvan for questioning, Batty is taken to the garda station in Waterford City. Clare tells me they will keep me informed, and I hear no more until six o'clock that evening.

'It's going very well.' Clare sounds in good spirits.

I have been driving, and I pull over to take the call. 'What does that mean?' I ask.

'So far, we've only put your charges to him,' she says. 'He is not admitting to them, but he isn't denying them either.'

'He's not?'

'Would you believe he has actually given us some details and information you hadn't provided?'

'I don't know what to make of that,' I tell her.

'He thinks he's clever and has started to talk a bit too much for his own good. We have to release him after twenty-four hours. I'll call you before that happens. Don't worry. We're well on track, I promise.'

I get a call at six the following morning. It is Clare again.

'We're releasing him,' she tells me. 'A file will be sent to the Director of Public Prosecutions today.'

'A file saying what?'

'All the information we've learned during the investigation of this case. Obviously, we're recommending it goes to trial, but that is up to the DPP. In the meantime, we'll be releasing Batty, but he will be advised not to leave town without letting us know.'

'Did he say anything else?'

'He has neither confirmed nor denied any of the charges.'

'So he said nothing?'

'Oh, he's said plenty. Sit tight, Stephanie. This is the first round. It's all still to play for.'

That doesn't give me a lot of comfort.

Team Batty

After Batty is arrested, questioned and then released, three months pass agonisingly slowly. Thankfully, I don't run in to him during this period – I don't know how I would cope if I bumped in to him. Clare and David keep in regular contact and are at pains to remind me that the DPP has the matter in hand.

'We have to wait until we receive the green light,' Clare insists to me one evening when I am feeling very low and just fed up with the whole thing.

'I don't understand what the hold-up is,' I moan. 'How difficult is it to say "yes, he did it" or "no, he didn't"? What's so complicated about that?'

'The process, as slow and labour-intensive as it might

seem, is there to protect everyone,' Clare reassures me. 'You wouldn't like it if the gardaí could just run around arresting whoever they felt like and sticking them in jail.'

'But the DPP doesn't even know me.' I sigh.

'That's the whole point. We present all the evidence to someone who has experience with the law and the investigative process, but who is completely detached and can look everything over with an objective eye. If they agree we have done our job properly and have collated enough viable, substantiated information, we can progress to the next stage.'

'Which is charging him?' I venture.

'Exactly. Just sit tight. I know it's hard, but everything is following the timeline I would have expected. It won't be long now.'

Batty is rearrested as he arrives to work a week later. This time he is brought to Dungarvan garda station. I get a call at twenty past nine from Clare to tell me that he is being arraigned in Dungarvan courthouse at ten that morning.

I am all afluster. I am a twenty-minute drive away in good traffic. Riccardo is off school, Deedee is at work, Angelo is in Clonmel getting a tyre mended, and I am just not ready.

I call everyone I can think of, but at such short notice no one is available to keep an eye on Riccardo. That said, he is twelve years old and not likely to go joy-riding or attempting to build a bomb in his bedroom, so I leave him at my parents' house and turn my car for Dungarvan.

Angelo calls en route, to inform me that he will meet me at the courthouse.

'You are not doing this alone,' he insists. 'I will be with you.'

We take a seat at the back of the room.

And we wait.

I am all on edge – this feels like a monumental moment, but I don't know how I am going to react when I see Batty under these circumstances. It doesn't feel real. Angelo takes my hand and we sit, side by side, waiting for the monster to be brought in.

At ten thirty the door opens and there he is.

He is handcuffed and between two female gardaí. He sees me but doesn't acknowledge my presence and is led slowly to the front of the room, where he sits. He looks smaller, somehow, in this place so full of import. For the first time he is not in control of what is going on, and there is the briefest of moments when I almost feel bad for him.

I don't know where that pity comes from – I can only think that, regardless of everything that has occurred, I never lost my humanity. The sadness is for my sister and her children and my parents and everyone I know who is going to be hurt by what is certain to follow.

I push the feeling aside because it does not help me now. I register that I am glad to see him in cuffs – it seems right and proper that he is – and I remind myself that he is here to face what he has done for the first time. Batty (and this is perhaps the only time I can say this) looks a bit shocked. He is pale and rumpled-looking, and he does not appear to be as cool as usual.

That makes me glad.

Five minutes later the door opens again, and Tisha and one of her and Batty's daughters (who is now in her thirties) come in. Batty looks back, and he and Tisha see one another. She nods at him, a gesture of 'are you all right'? He nods back ('I'm OK'), and I see (and again, this is the only time I can report this) that there are tears in his eyes, and he is shaking ever so slightly.

I would love to be able to say that this is a sign of remorse, of my brother-in-law realising the error of his ways, but don't be fooled for a moment – it is no such thing. This is Batty feeling sorry for himself. Remember how I mentioned he would always cower and go quiet when he and Tisha had an argument or when he was being pulled up on something?

This is another example of that: *poor me, I don't deserve this.*

It makes me feel a little bit sick.

Batty's daughter begins to cry, and one of the gardaí gets up and goes to comfort the girl. Batty's solicitor also gets up. They take her outside for a few minutes, then everyone returns and we resume waiting.

Batty's case is called about midday, and it is all gone through very quickly.

The judge asks if the case will be formally heard in Dublin, and the lawyer confirms that it will.

'And this is all relating to historic cases of sexual abuse?' the judge asks.

'Allegedly, judge,' Batty's solicitor responds.

'Anything to add before I proceed?'

'Can I request that my client's postal address not be read into the record?'

Myself and Angelo exchange looks. This seems odd. I ask about it afterwards, and Clare (who cannot be with me as she is teaching in the garda college in Templemore) tells me that it is unusual, but not unheard of – keeping his address out of the record is intended to protect the safety and privacy of his family.

'Noted. OK, let's get on with it then.'

Batty is asked to stand and is informed that he is being bound to the peace and will have to present himself at Dungarvan garda station twice a week until his case is heard. He is to hand over his passport, and a bail bond of one thousand euro is set (this irritates me because it means he will get the money back once his case is heard – I would have liked to have seen the cash given to one of the charities that help survivors of sexual abuse).

When this is all finished, Batty is told to sit down, which he does, his hand pressed to his chest as if he is having trouble breathing or his heart is racing. But he looks relieved, too.

The court begins to clear, and after five minutes or so Batty goes past us and out the doors.

'We'll give them five minutes and then we'll go,' I tell Angelo. 'I really need a cigarette.'

'Five minutes,' Angelo agrees.

When we exit the court, Batty is still outside. He is in a cluster with Tisha, his solicitor and his daughter. They are all talking furiously, and Angelo and I slip quietly past and make for our respective vehicles.

As I drive home, what jars more than anything else about the whole experience is that, in spite of everything, my sister chose to be at his side and to offer comfort to him. She could have stayed away.

She could have sat with me.

It makes me even more determined.

Central Criminal Court, Dublin

November 2018

Take Him Down

I want to get out of the Central Criminal Court as quickly as I can now Justice Creedon has left the stand. I need to look up at the sky, feel the air on my face and breathe. As soon as she is gone, I stand up and make a bolt towards the door.

'Where do you think you're going?' Clare asks me.

'Anywhere so long as it's out of here,' I mutter.

'Not yet,' she says. 'I want you to watch him being taken away.'

'I don't care any more,' I say, probably with more anger than it warrants. 'I've had enough.'

'You'll be glad you did,' she says. 'Believe me, girl, this is an important part of it. He is being taken to *prison*, Stephanie. You owe it to yourself to see him go.'

Begrudgingly, I sit back down and fix my eyes on Batty.

He is still seated and speaking calmly to his barristers,

who seem slightly more agitated than he is. They are informing him in hushed voices of something (I wonder if they are discussing a possible appeal or some other tactic to lessen his sentence), and while he appears politely interested, I know by him that his head is elsewhere.

And who could blame him?

My brother-in-law is about to be carted off to prison.

Within the space of the next minute or so, Batty is going to make the transition from free man, able to come and go as he wishes, to being incarcerated, a part of the prison system. He is destined for a place most of us are taught to fear, where a key will turn in the lock behind him and he will no longer be in charge, no more the big man, never again a person people look up to and admire.

He is going to be forever branded by the crime he committed and the sentence he will serve.

He *should* be frightened, or at the very least anxious, but he seems perfectly calm and comfortable. The barristers finish whatever final pieces of advice they are offering and Batty stands and stretches. Two men, supporters of Batty's, get up from a few rows behind him and make their way to his side.

I know these men well – they are well respected, and I cannot understand why they would want to be seen supporting Batty. They shake his hand and tell him they wish him well.

'Take care of yourself, now,' one says, placing a hand on his shoulder. 'Keep your head down, d'ye hear me?'

'I'll be grand.' Batty smiles. 'Sure, I'll be talking to you again soon.'

I marvel at this. Does he think they'll be visiting him, or does he expect to be out? He seems so content, it could be either.

Another man joins the little group. They exchange a few words and the third man, who has not been slow about letting me know how appalled he is at my pressing charges against a man so upstanding in the community as Bartholomew Prendergast, throws me a look of complete disdain.

I stare right back. I have allowed people like him to intimidate me in the past, but not now. Not today. I hold his gaze and, to my delight, after only a few seconds he looks away. Not so brave after all.

A couple of gardaí come up to Batty, and without further ado he is taken out a door on the right side of the room. It closes behind him, and he is gone from my view.

'Is that it?' I ask Clare.

'It is,' she says. 'He's away. He'll probably spend tonight in Mountjoy and it'll be off to the Midlands Prison tomorrow.'

'So he's gone?'

'He has been taken away to jail,' Clare says. 'He is a guest of the nation, and you, Stephanie Hickey, are free to get on with the rest of your life.'

I don't have the heart to tell her that I don't feel free yet at all.

West Waterford

2018

The Viking Half-Marathon

I arrive in Carriganore on the morning of the half-marathon. It is mid-January and it is cold and damp and I'm freezing. I have layers of clothes on (skins, shorts, my running scarf, my hat, a sweatshirt, several T-shirts) and I'm not in a good headspace. Angelo was supposed to be here to cheer me on, but he has gotten lost and is now at the other end of the route, at the Waterford IT campus, and this has thrown me off.

Eamonn Cashin, my trainer, is trying to talk me into a better frame of mind when a familiar figure cuts through the crowd. It's Colm, the coach of our running group from back home.

'What are you doing here?' I ask grumpily.

'I'm going to be running with you,' he grins, 'for the company.'

'No, you're not!' I snap at him. 'You're too fast. I'll be worn out trying to keep up with you.'

'You don't get it,' Eamonn says. 'This is all about you – you set the pace and Colm will follow your lead.'

'And I'll carry your water bottle,' Colm suggests.

I realise what is going on – Eamonn, in an act of great kindness, has understood that a lot of my security when it comes to running is rooted in the Ballymacarbery gang. By having Colm run alongside me, he is giving me the athletic equivalent of a comfort blanket. I feel my mood lift slightly.

'And you're sure about this?' I ask Colm. 'It'll destroy your completion time.'

'There's always next year,' he says, and I feel a surge of gratitude for this gentle, selfless man.

The race begins, and the first thing that hits me is the crowd. There are more than three thousand people running, and I feel hemmed in and suffocated. I'm used to the countryside and a small group of companions (and more and more I've been running alone in the early morning). This feels as if I am trying to jog through the middle of a rock concert.

I consider just giving up there and then, but I glance over at Colm, who is calmly shadowing me, and I think: *how will I feel if I actually do this? If I finish?* And I know I have to keep going. I tell myself that the crowd will disperse as we put some distance between us and the starting line, and I keep trudging forward.

I go to that place I always go to when I run, deep inside my head. It's me and the road and the beating of my heart. The world streams by me and my limbs work their magic and the miles sweep by.

I hit the wall at about six miles, and I hit it hard.

'I'm in trouble,' I tell Colm.

'Take this,' he says, and passes me a tube of isotonic energy gel. 'It'll give you a boost.'

The supplement hits me, I feel my body's engine rev and suddenly I'm warm. Sweat beads form on my forehead, and before I know it, I'm shedding layers, passing items of clothing to Colm.

With each quarter mile, another piece of my armour comes off, and I feel lighter and freer and stronger. It is as if I am losing slices of myself, and it feels so good. As each one comes away, I hand it to my coach and friend, and he accepts it with a smile.

That he is taking on my burden is not lost on me. We both know it, but there is no need to say anything. It is all part of the unspoken language of the run, of the special thing this race is for us.

At the ten-mile mark we hit a steep hill. I am wearing the singlet from the Ballymacarbery Couch to 5K race, (though we'd actually run 6K) and as we start up the incline, I hear someone on the sidelines say, 'Look – it's one of the Ballymac girls. She'll power up this – sure aren't they well used to hills?'

'Are you going to accept that challenge?' Colm winks.

I nod, and the two of us make a burst upwards – where I got the strength I will never know, but we charge through the other runners and scale that hill as if it was barely there.

We pass the Holy Cross pub on the Cork Road and turn back down for the return into Carriganore and the finish line. It is relatively flat, but my issues with a level landscape resurface, and I'm not sure I can make it. Colm gives me another energy boost.

'I want you to finish strong,' he tells me as I consume the gel. 'Take some water and ease back. When I tell you to go, we're going to really put the foot down, OK?'

Both Colm and Eamonn have prepared me for this: in training, we would do a mile at a virtual sprint, but then slow down to close to a walk for another mile, then back to a sprint again. It's about building reserves that you can summon when you need them. Eamonn often scolds me for being a bit lazy – I know I have power banked inside me that I don't usually use, and he consistently tells me I need to push myself, to go that extra mile.

Maybe it's something to do with the abuse – I'm afraid to go to those very deep places in case I find something in there I don't like.

So at a gentle jog, Colm and I begin the toil back into Carriganore. I can hear the announcers calling out the names of the runners crossing the finish line.

'Five minutes,' Colm tells me. 'Five more minutes and you have it done.'

I look at him in wonderment. 'Really?'

'Really.'

I shake my head in disbelief.

'You've only been in serious training with a coach for a wet weekend, and you're about to complete a half-marathon,' Colm tells me. 'You should be so proud of yourself.'

I don't know what to say.

'Are you ready to make a break for the finish?' he asks.

I peel off the final T-shirt I have on over my running gear and hand it to him, passing on the last of the dead weight. He adds it to the bundle he has been carrying for all these miles. I feel so light now. So free.

'I'm ready.'

The last five hundred yards are a blur. I can hear my name being called and I know I've completed the race and I sink to the ground, down on my hands and knees, thinking again and again: *I've done it, I've done it!*

I would stay right there, except a steward sternly asks me to move (I have actually collapsed right in the path of the other runners).

He can't wreck my buzz, though. I have never felt so proud of myself.

It is a feeling I will try to summon again and again in the run-up to the court case.

Lights in the Darkness

I've been having the nightmares again.

In my dream I seem to wake up and my bed is in the middle of a sea of blackness and, no matter which way I look, I can see no light. The dark is so complete I cannot even detect the floor or the ceiling. All about me is a frigid cold and my breath comes in a cloud with each exhalation.

I know where I am.

I am inside myself, in the deep place where my most awful demons hide. This is the part of me I have been running from since my early teens – this is what I have tried so long to avoid. I go to pull the blankets over my head to block out the horror when I sense movement above me, and looking up, there he is: his huge, sagging body is suspended in the blackness above, lit by an inner luminescence. Lank, drooping hair hangs about his bloated face, and hands that are always seeking reach out for me imploringly. Hunger and desire radiate from him with the shimmer of heat that can never be extinguished, and like a spider suspended on a strand of silk, he begins to lower himself upon me, the movement slow, steady and irrevocable.

I scream and lash out but it does no good.

It never did any good.

I've been having this same dream for a long time now. It started recurring about a year before we took Batty to court, and I went to visit my GP.

I went right away, because it got so I was afraid to sleep at all.

'Do you want me to recommend a psychiatrist?'

I looked at him in disgust. 'Psychiatrists do no good from what I can tell,' I snapped. 'Give me something that'll knock me out so heavily I won't dream.'

I should probably explain my reluctance to deal with counsellors and psychiatrists.

After Batty was sent to see a psychiatrist, we were all told he was 'cured', but I knew better from bitter, painful experience.

As a result, I have no faith whatsoever in psychiatry. I understand completely that some people swear by it, and I am of the opinion that you should take your comfort where you can. For me, though, the only thing that ever brought me comfort was running.

My GP struggled with this concept, however. 'I can't give you a sedative,' he said apologetically.

'Why the hell not?'

'Because I'm not certain you need it. Has the running stopped helping?'

'I'm sleeping now, which is an improvement. But when I sleep, I dream.'

'I see. Can I suggest another more *holistic* approach?'

'You're losing me, doctor.'

'Help yourself by helping others.'

'I still don't follow.'

He reached behind him and pulled a flier off the notice board on the wall. It was from an agency that employed home helpers for the elderly and disabled.

'They're looking for people to do some part-time work. It's not too heavy – a lot of it just involves spending time with people who are housebound, maybe cooking some meals and doing a bit of light housework. I think it might help you get out of your own head a little.'

I told him I'd think about it.

That weekend the nightmares woke me almost on the hour and by Sunday I could see no point in going to bed at all. Finally, the dreams stopped, but as the court case loomed closer, they came back. I suppose I know why: I became terrified: what if they don't believe me and he is found innocent? What will the neighbours think? How will my family see me if I am humiliated at this, the last hurdle? In my dream, Batty is hanging over me, waiting to strike, and that is how it feels in my waking life, too.

I know that the approaching legal battle is one I started, but I am now wondering if I have made a huge mistake.

Knowing that I need to find something to distract me from my sleeping and waking nightmares, I dig out the flier my GP gave me and call the agency. They ask me to go for an interview. I have good references and they offer me work on the spot, subject to garda vetting.

My first job is with a man with an intellectual disability called Larry. During the week he lives in a residential community, and I pick him up at the weekends and take him to town. We have dinner and talk and I enjoy spending time with him. It makes me feel good to be helping someone, and I understand that, in his innocent, open-hearted way, he is helping me, too.

I get a call asking if I would be interested in being part of a three-person team working one night a week in a retirement home for an order of nuns, the Presentation Sisters. I respond that I am not religious, but it seems that is not part of the job description, so I agree to give it a go.

I am surprised at the sense of calm I experience working with these women. Every evening when I walk through the door to begin my shift, I have no idea what the next twelve hours will bring, but there is something serene and beautiful and powerfully feminine about them.

I am well aware of the bad press the religious orders have

received in Ireland in recent years, and I have no intention of being an apologist for them and their worst excesses. But I believe people should be judged by their individual actions rather than by those of any collective, and all I see from these particular women is warmth, kindness and absolute acceptance.

I have seen them at their best, laughing, chatting, joking and having fun – they surprise me with their sense of humour, their enjoyment of sport and music, their capacity to tell bawdy stories and poke fun at one another.

And I have sat with them through their worst – I have been privileged to be with them in their final moments (five have passed on to the next world while in my care). Each of them faced death with courage and calm acceptance. Never, in all that time, have I seen them be anything other than deeply caring to me and to one another.

As the court case looms closer – we are coming into March and the date has been set for August – I know I have to tell Anne, the Mother Superior, about Batty and the fact that Deedee and I have waived our anonymity. One of the things that amazes me about the sisters is how up-to-the-minute they are when it comes to current affairs – they watch the news every day without fail and read all the papers, broadsheet and tabloid. I don't want them to switch on the television and be confronted with my mug staring back at them.

Mother Anne is in her early seventies, a handsome woman with the upright bearing you would expect from someone in the military. She sits me down in her office and listens without interrupting as I tearfully explain that I am about to be thrust into the spotlight and that the publicity is likely to be scandalous and upsetting.

I tell her that I hope this will not affect my working with her and her sisters, whom I have come to value as dear friends, but that I would understand if she felt such exposure made my position untenable.

When I am finished, Anne takes my hands in hers and tells me that there is no question whatsoever of my stopping working with the order. She tells me that she cannot imagine what I have been through and that I am to consider the nuns my family for as long as I need them.

Through the stress and trauma of the trial, I find my work with the sisters a calm island amid all the obstacles I face. It is one of the most important lessons of my life: sometimes you find friends in the place you least expect.

I cherish them as true lights in the darkness. Their warmth and kindness cut a swathe through the bad times and showed me the way home.

Ultraman

I am probably insufferable after I finish the Viking half-marathon. I bring my medal with me everywhere and will take it out at the least provocation. It is, I tell anyone who will listen, the biggest accomplishment of my life so far. (My children point out that motherhood should rank quite highly, too, but I assure them there is no competition – the half-marathon trumps everything!)

After a lengthy break (which Eamonn and Colm insist on because they know how physically draining such a long race can be), I am back to my regular morning jaunts and my evening runs with my friends in Ballymacarbery.

In the months leading up to the trial I notch up more races. I begin to do quite a few with Danielle, my daughter. She is a professional dancer, and she runs to keep up her fitness and stamina. She will call to let me know she has booked us in somewhere and to put the date in my diary. We'll do the race and make a day out of it.

I love these mother–daughter excursions. That one of my kids can share a passion that has come to mean so much to me brings me great joy.

We do the Mallow 10K together, the John Treacy 10 mile in Dungarvan and several lesser-known runs around the country when Danielle is travelling to those locations to dance.

Running has become a big part of who I am – I cannot see what the shape of my life would be without it.

One day in April I receive a call from Colm. He asks if I would like to go for a run with him that evening. It's not my usual night, but I get the sense he wants to talk about something, so I agree to go along. We end up running along the wooded road above Clonmel, and when we reach the point where the whole countryside opens up before us, he motions for us to stop.

'I want to ask you a favour,' he says as we both take some water and feel the sweat drying into our backs. 'I know you have a hell of a lot going on at the moment, but I don't know who else to ask.'

'Anything you need,' I say, and I mean it. I owe this man. Maybe more than I can ever repay.

'I want to do a run for cancer,' he says. 'You know I've lost people dear to me to it.'

'Of course I do.'

'I'd like to raise some money for cancer research,' he continues.

'That's a great idea,' I agree. 'Do you want to organise a 10K? We could get all the local girls to run. Feck it, we could do another half-marathon!'

'That's not what I mean,' Colm says. 'I know what I'm going to do. I want to run fifty miles. In one day.'

What Colm is proposing is a kind of ultra-marathon. It is considered an extreme sport and is outrageously tough. My coach is one of the fittest and strongest men I know, but this will be a huge challenge.

'I want to start in Carriganore, where the half-marathon you did finished, and run all the way back to Ballymacarbery,' he says.

'What do you want me to do?' I ask him. 'I mean, I'd love to be able to do the whole thing with you, but it's a bit out of my league!'

'I want you to join me for the last leg of it,' he says. 'The final seven miles. I know I'll be in a bad way by then, and I'm going to need all the friends I can get to help me on.'

He turns to look at me then, and I know he's scared. This is a huge task he's proposing. Colm has never asked me for anything in all the time I have known him. All he has ever done is give.

'I'll be there,' I tell him. 'And I'll help you get the word out. Raise some publicity.'

He grins his thanks and, without another word, we begin the run back home.

Colm's fifty-mile ultra will be one of the most emotional runs I have ever done.

The Language of Abuse

When you go public with a case like this, it changes people's perceptions of who you are.

In the Nire Valley I am Stephanie Hickey, Tommy Hickey's daughter. For as long as I remember, I was known as a dancer, a mother, a separated wife. I am in no doubt some people thought of me as Batty Prendergast's sister-in-law (people would have seen me going about with him in his van). People would have known me from Tisha's salon as the girl who washed the hair, too, so I have to accept that part of my identity will always be entwined with them.

I am known as the woman in a relationship with the Italian man – the outsider setting up house with another outsider.

I am OK with that. Being an outsider is not all bad. But it is not all of what I am, either.

In more recent years I am known for being involved in the community: an active member of Neighbourhood Watch, a runner in the Ballymacarbery group and a carer for the Presentation nuns.

Which makes me an insider, too.

Human beings are complex creatures.

When I made the decision to press charges, I had to add another role to all these others: the role of *victim*. Victim of abuse, victim of rape, victim of *familial sexual molestation*.

It has never occurred to me before how powerful language can be, but the word 'victim' hits me particularly hard. I hate the connotations it carries. It makes me feel like something that has been used up and tossed aside, and that is not a way I like to look at myself.

A victim is a pathetic thing, a helpless thing. A victim is beaten and broken and unable to help herself. A victim is tears and cries and potential brought to a grinding halt.

I hate it because I see there is truth in it.

I have wanted to just stop many times, and there were moments when I felt like tears in a human shape, but I will not let that define me. I believe I have surpassed the pain and the sorrow and the wretchedness and risen above it.

I know what I am.

I am a *survivor*.

Yet even that is a complicated and layered term. It is a word I have used, in this book, to describe Bartholomew Prendergast and I am not oblivious to that.

I want to take this opportunity to draw a distinction: while I am a true survivor, Batty has a *survival instinct*.

Batty has learned to camouflage himself among healthy people, and he has taught himself to be charming and to play all sorts of games to win over the weak and the vulnerable. He is furtive and dangerous.

Survival brings no joy for him – he has not earned it. He has cheated fate and continued to do so until it finally caught up with him. Every day he evaded capture was another day of stress and worry that he might be caught the next.

I am a different being entirely.

I have known pain and fear and I have not allowed myself to be cowed by it. When despair hovered above me like a poisonous cloud, I did not submit: I held my breath and pushed through until I came to the clear air on the other side. When the monster stood at the door of my room and forced me to follow, I bided my time and waited until I found a chink in its armour and then I struck. There were moments when the shadows seemed to be all there was, but I never ceased moving forward, one step at a time. I continued until I found the light again.

I am not a victim.

I am a survivor.

I have earned that title and I bear it proudly.

STEPHANIE AND DEEDEE

WEST WATERFORD AND DUBLIN, THE LAST SIX MONTHS OF 2018

Enough

I spend the four months waiting for Batty to be sentenced simply trying to keep busy. Eamonn Cashin works out a regime that will keep me fit, both physically and mentally, and I throw myself into it with deep gratitude.

He does not give me a second to dwell on my anxieties and worries (a voice at the back of my mind keeps telling me that when we finally go back to court, Batty will be released on time served, and it will have all been for nothing), giving me targets I must meet at various points in the day. He texts me first thing in the morning to remind me to go for my early run. He sends me messages at midday wanting to know what protein I am taking for my lunch. He even wants to know how much I'm sleeping.

If I leave my thoughts to their own devices for even a second, I go to a dark place, so Eamonn's kindness is much appreciated. He drives me like a workhorse, which is exactly what I need.

The sisters have been amazingly kind to me, quietly asking every now and again if I am all right and assuring me that Deedee and I are in their prayers. They never press me and they never pry, just make sure I feel nurtured and cared for.

Everyone in the community has been following the case. As Deedee and I waived our anonymity, reporters have been in the court, and as sentence has not been passed, they can only report on the fact that the trial is happening, but in a small area like the Nire, that is all people need.

Every time I go to the shops, people are asking me what I think he's going to get or what sentence I believe would be fair. My answer is always that I don't know and that it is up to the judge, but of course I want to tell them that, as far as I am concerned, they should lock him up and throw away the key.

It's not all good. Sometimes people are rude or abrasive. A man I barely know pauses in a pub one night to tell me I should be ashamed of myself. A woman I thought was a friend blanks me in the street. A relative I had always cared for tells my mother he is disowning me.

No matter how many positive responses I get, it is the negative stuff I focus on.

As sentencing draws closer I am reduced to a bundle of nerves. I can barely eat or sleep.

November finally arrives, and we all prepare for a return

to Dublin and the Central Criminal Court. We have our tickets bought for the journey, outfits packed and arrangements made, but on the Friday before we are to travel, I receive a message – the case has been postponed, as the judge is unavailable.

All the old fears return.

What does this mean? Will the whole thing have to be retried? What if they don't find him guilty a second time? Maybe it's all been a mistake?

Damien Tiernan is a journalist covering the story for RTÉ, Ireland's national broadcaster. Damien has been very kind to Deedee and me, and he tells me to relax.

'I've been covering court cases for years,' he says. 'This happens more often than you'd think. My guess is you'll be called the same day next week. Sit tight and you'll see.'

He is right, of course, but that week crawls by at a snail's pace. Every day stretches out like a year, and when Friday arrives I spend it checking my phone every thirty seconds, convinced another message will arrive to inform me that sentencing has been adjourned again. But no such message comes, and on Monday, 3 December we pack onto the train and travel to Dublin in a group: me, Angelo and my children, Deedee, Ciaran and her gang, as well as my brothers and their families.

I think, as we jump and judder our way out of Thurles, that people looking might think we were on our way to a wedding or a birthday party. That makes me smile in a sad kind of way.

As we troop over Liam Mellows Bridge and I see the Four Courts looming above us, I pray that this will be the last day I ever spend in this place. I hold Angelo's hand tight, and I know he is thinking the exact same thing.

Getting into the building seems to take forever today. The pedestrian crossing is interminably slow, and when we get to the metal detector everyone has to pass through, I seem to set it off about fifty times, and I go back through and take off another ring and root around for change I had forgotten I had. The garda is very patient, but I am losing patience with myself!

Finally, we are in, and I go to the green room to change into my suit.

Bizarrely, the morning whizzes by, and before I even finish my second cup of tea, we are called.

The courtroom is exactly as it was before. I sit in the same seat, and Batty, dressed in a blue suit (with what I am starting to think of as his lucky plastic bag held tightly), sits exactly where he has always sat.

Justice Creedon comes in and the charges are read yet again. I grit my teeth and look right ahead and try not to listen. When this process is complete, the judge begins to speak, but it is legalese and I don't understand any of it.

Clare whispers that this is normal. 'There's a kind of statement she has to make before passing sentence,' she explains. 'It's kind of like giving her credentials, telling us why she's allowed to do this. It'll be over in a minute or two.'

Justice Creedon finishes her preamble and looks at

Batty. 'Bartholomew Prendergast, I want you to keep in mind that the crimes which have you in my court today carry a mandatory life sentence. I am, however, granted some leeway when it comes to sexual offences, and I am inclined to give you some small credit for your guilty plea, albeit offered at such a late hour and at the urging of your counsel. I am also going to operate a little leniency in that you do not appear to have reoffended in some time.'

As the judge is speaking, she is knocking years off the sentence. Life, in this instance, means fourteen years (which I find very disappointing). I don't remember the exact wording or how much came off for each item on her list, but I remember she reached ten years and stopped.

'That leaves us with a ten-year sentence, Mr Prendergast. Now I am going to give you a chance to lessen this a little bit more. I will suspend eighteen months if you attend a programme of psychological therapy for sex offenders while you are in prison. I am aware that these programmes are not popular with prisoners, but I want you to be aware that if you do not attend, those eighteen months will remain on your docket.'

My family are all looking at me, trying to work out what I'm feeling. I'm still looking at Batty. He does not seem happy and he does not seem sad.

'Are you clear on that point, Mr Prendergast?'

He mumbles something that I assume is an affirmative answer.

'I want to iterate here that you have had a profound and

negative impact on the lives of your victims, who were all left feeling fear, guilt and shame. I'd like you to think about that when you consider whether or not to avail of therapy.'

She pauses, as if she is waiting for Batty to respond, but he doesn't. Almost with a shrug, she says, 'The sentence is so given,' and, banging her gavel, it is done.

Batty's supporters rush up and talk to him, shaking his hand again, but I barely notice. I am being hugged on all sides (I don't even know who is embracing me half the time), and this time, I don't see Batty being taken away.

I don't care.

The man who abused me, my sister and my friend has been sent away for ten years. I fought and I won. It was frightening and horrible and exhausting but I kept on going, one foot in front of the other, until it was done.

As I stand in the court and feel the absence of his presence, I experience a sense of disorientation.

The court dissolves around me, and suddenly I am looking down upon myself from above. I realise it is thirteen-year-old me, huddled in the back of Batty Prendergast's van, and he is looming over her prone figure. I see that frozen, terrified child and, in my mind's eye, I reach down and take her hand and whisper to her, 'I've got you, Stephanie. I've got you.'

And in that moment of horror, she takes some small comfort.

I did it for her. I did it for me.

I don't know if ten years truly balances what Batty Prendergast did, but today it will have to be enough.

Changing the System

The press have gathered. Damien Tiernan is acting as a kind of MC – he has told them Deedee and I are fragile, that we have had a rough few years since the process began. We are not to be mobbed or rushed by them. He assures us we will not be bombarded with questions – he will ask what needs to be asked and the journalists can record our answers.

I realise that I really want to speak. I want to tell them how it has been for me. I believe this is an important part of why Deedee and I waived anonymity. How we experienced the process is something we want to share, so others can know what it is like and not be afraid.

Damien brings us all to the hall at the front of the Central

Criminal Court. A crowd of journalists is gathered – I cannot tell you exactly how many, but there is a sea of faces and each one seems to be clutching a microphone. I hold Deedee's hand. Damien brings us to a particular spot (the light and acoustics are good here, he tells us) and this is where we hold our press conference.

Deedee speaks first. Damien asks the questions, going over the whole experience, from the sentencing, to how she felt giving her victim impact statement, to how she is feeling now it's all over.

We stand there and the cameras are all click, click, clicking, and I wonder how people who are open to this kind of scrutiny all the time cope. I am proud of Deedee. She speaks slowly and clearly and I think she is very brave.

Damien then directs the same set of questions to me. I answer, but there is something I have been waiting to say, and I am determined to speak my truth.

I get my chance when he asks me about Batty's lawyers wanting to have character references read into the record.

'I want to say something about how victims are treated by the system,' I say. 'This entire process has been gruelling. There have been periods when it was dragged out much longer than it needed to be. I would like the Irish government to consider sitting down with victims and hearing how they best feel the legal process should work. Is it really necessary for us to sit in court and have to hear back what was done to us again and again and again? Does it serve anyone that we be made endure discussions about character references for those who ruined our lives? There is only one word for that – it is degrading. By the time a case like this arrives in court, the victims have already been through enough. For them to have to tolerate conversations that suggest their abuser is actually not a bad fella at all is just incomprehensible to me.'

Damien stands back and allows me to speak. I am grateful for that.

'Sex offenders are experts at hiding in plain sight. They lie and they conspire and they groom their victims and their victims' families. How does a character reference, which only shows the mask they use to hide their true selves, enlighten anyone as to their true character? The *abuse* is the mark of their true character.'

There are more questions, but I am happy. I have said what I needed to.

In the coming days and weeks, I give interviews to all the major radio stations, and the case is covered in every single newspaper. I do an hour-long interview on WLR FM, the Waterford local radio station.

I am delighted to be able to tell my story to anyone who wants to hear it, but that answer, outside the court on the afternoon Batty was sent away, is the speech I am most proud of.

Being a Daughter
(and a bit more about how
abuse messes with your head)

We buried my father, Thomas Hickey, on 10 April 2019, just before I started work on this book. There are no words to describe the gap he leaves behind, so I'm not even going to try to express that loss. Instead, I'm going to tell you what kind of a man he was and what kind of a father.

Daddy was one of the most affectionate, warm-hearted and good-spirited people I have ever met, and I was always his pet.

It's probably because I'm the youngest, but he never seemed able to see me as anything other than the baby.

There were times when I loved this and definitely took advantage of it – my brothers and sisters would tell me that I was absolutely his favourite. And, as an adult, if I needed him, he would come running, whether it was to move furniture or just to be a listening ear.

There were occasions, though, when I was younger, when I resented his involvement in every aspect of my life. It seemed he was making decisions for me or disempowering me. It's hard to feel like you're in charge of your own destiny when your father is still telling you what you should do and offering to make all the arrangements.

I now know that he was taking the parts of my burden that he was able to carry. For a long time I was angry about that meeting in Tisha and Batty's house and about him involving Father Crowley. I felt I should have been consulted or even told about the decision and the thought process behind it when I was older. For a long time I wondered if they guessed what Batty was doing – did they realise I was in harm's way?

But I have come to understand that people just didn't grasp what sexual abuse was, in those days – they could not grasp the appalling impact it has on victims' lives.

I believe Daddy did come to get a sense of it, though.

I think he knew something wasn't right with me long before I told him, and that he was doing his best to let me know he cared and was there for me. Daddy was an old-fashioned, traditional man, and he showed us he loved us through his actions. Among the other fathers in and around

Touraneena, he was unusual in that he was very physically demonstrative – he was always cuddling us, and I can still remember those bear-hugs and how safe they made me feel.

One of the things that hurt me most about the abuse was the wedge it drove between me and my father. As soon as it happened, I felt different, like I wasn't his little girl any more. As if, for the first time, there was something I couldn't share with him, and that altered our relationship. I felt like I was lying to him, as if my involvement in the abuse made me a traitor to everything our family stood for.

I would feel myself freezing up when my dad went to put his arms around me, and it took all my strength not to let him sense that I was pulling away, although I believe he did notice a change in me. I never blamed him for not protecting me – what could he have done? I blamed myself for not being a better daughter. For letting him down.

He found the court case very hard, particularly how it fractured relationships within our family. There were times when I know he wished it would all go away, but he never gave voice to these feelings. He stood by my decision. He knew I was doing it for him as much as for myself.

Batty's fingerprints were all over my relationship with my mother, too. She was a very different person to Dad. Mammy expressed her affection by always having wonderful things for us to eat, by always being present in the home and through driving me and my friends here, there and everywhere without a word of complaint. She would often pack ten of us into the car (no one cared about the insurance implications in those days) and head off to a match or for a picnic somewhere.

Mammy doted on Batty. He charmed everyone and he paid special attention to Mammy. He would always arrive at the house with some little gift for her, and his first smile and greeting as he strode through the door was always to her.

I think he knew that, in our house, Mammy was where the power lay. Daddy was gentle and a bit of a people-pleaser: he hated conflict and arguments and would go out of his way to make sure peace and harmony reigned. Mammy was much more combative and was never slow to put someone in their place if they set a foot wrong. The predator in Bartholomew Prendergast recognised the alpha female in our den, and he made it his mission to win her over and to get beside her.

And I want you to understand that this is central to what abusers do. They groom and they manipulate and they worm their way into your affections until you find it unbelievable that they could be the monster they truly are.

I can see them now, Batty and my mother, sitting opposite one another in our living room in the renovated schoolhouse, him telling her one of his funny, rambling stories (in which he was always the hero) and her hanging on his every word. She's probably nibbling a biscuit from an expensive box he's brought along and sipping from a cup of tea he's insisted on making ('You sit down, Kathleen

– no one ever looks after you in this house,' he'll have cooed at her). And she is enraptured by him. Tisha will be smiling beatifically in the corner, taking it all in, and Mammy will say to her as they leave what a good man she has. What a wonderful son-in-law.

My mother was in the early stages of dementia during the trial, but she was lucid enough to know what was going on. It hurt her to the core to know a predator had connived its way into her den. I watched her moods veer from anger to heartbreak, sometimes in the space of a single sentence.

There were times when that anger was directed at Batty, but others when it was aimed at me. And that hurt.

What hope was there for me?

Time, however, has proved a great healer.

As the final work was being done on this book, Angelo, Riccardo and I moved back into the schoolhouse to live with my mother again and to look after her. It is my privilege to be able to share this time with her.

The other night, she held my hand as I put her to bed and told me she was proud of me.

And I think I knew what she was talking about.

Life-Changing

I am in a large supermarket in Clonmel doing some shopping. My head is completely focused on the task at hand, but as always there are half a dozen other dialogues running in the back of my mind at the same time, other jobs I know I need to get to at some stage before going home. Danielle is sitting with Mammy, and I know she is perfectly capable of taking care of her, but I remind myself that I must check in with her before I go to the convent (I still work there once a week, simply because I enjoy it so much).

I always pick up a little treat for the sisters, and that is what I am looking for when I feel a tap on the shoulder.

'You're her, aren't you?'

I turn to see a woman perhaps five or six years younger

than me. She is about my own height and very glamorously dressed in the most fashionable clothes – a pastel-coloured business suit over which she has a short jacket. I can tell she looks after herself: she has a strong build and her blonde hair is well cut and perfectly styled.

She is beautiful, but I can see she is upset and anxious about something.

'I suppose that depends on who you think I am,' I say, trying to force a smile.

'You're the woman in the papers,' she says. 'I heard you and your sister on the radio.'

I nod. 'Yes. I'm Stephanie.'

She seems to be summing me up, and I wait to see if this is going to be one of those unpleasant experiences, the type where she tells me I was asking for what I got or that I have ruined a good man's life.

I've heard it all before, and I know the best thing to do is just let it wash over me. Every word will resonate in my head later, but I always try to remind myself: Batty is locked up and I am out in the world, living my life.

Words can't hurt me.

But instead she says, 'Can I give you a hug?'

Suddenly, I see she is crying, and instinctively I put my arms around her.

'I ... I just want to thank you,' she says, her voice rough with tears.

'For what?' I ask.

'He used to come to my room at night when I was eleven,'

she whispers in my ear. 'He told me I would die if I ever told anyone, so I never did.'

I wish we weren't in the middle of the supermarket. This is not the right place for this kind of conversation, but sometimes, you have to just go with it.

She steps back, and even though the tears are still running down her cheeks, she is smiling. 'I heard you and your sister on the radio. You were so strong and so brave. That night, I went to the police myself. He's old now, but he's still alive. And he has grandchildren.'

I feel tears coming to my own eyes and I hug her tight all over again.

'I never would have gone if I hadn't heard your story,' she says. 'Thank you for doing what you did. For all of us.'

And then she disappears into the crowd of early-evening shoppers.

It is people like that woman who make it worthwhile.

A New Sense of Self

It's going to sound like a funny thing to say, but it feels weird when I realise the case is over. In some ways, that feels like a loss, too, because I have connected with so many people who have become important to me. These are people who have gotten to know me in ways most never will, because I have been forced to share intimate parts of myself with them, and allow myself to be vulnerable. I'm talking here about the gardaí who helped me and showed such kindness, and my legal team who helped to guide me through the maze of the courts system; I've even grown close to some of the journalists who covered the case, particularly Damien Tiernan and Eamon Keane. So many of these people have become friends to me and to Deedee.

I feel a strong urge to keep in contact, and in fairness to Damien, he still rings occasionally to see how I'm doing.

But I also know that this is a chapter in my story that I need to turn the page on. There is nothing to be gained by dwelling on the past and reliving old pain and resentment.

But there is also something I need to do that is harder still. I need to reshape my sense of who I am around the wounded, damaged bit. You see, I took that hurt, frightened Stephanie, that teenager who was trapped and terrified, and I showed her to the world. I can't pretend she doesn't exist anymore, I have to own her. And that means I have to find a way to make her a part of who I am now.

And that has perhaps been the most difficult part of all this because it involved a lot of soul-searching. I have spent long hours pondering how to move on in my life (writing this book was a part of the process), and throughout it all I came to understand that the only way I could ever find the path that would lead to my future was to embrace all of who I am, including that hurt teenage girl.

So despite any misgivings I may have had, I have learned to love her. That wasn't easy, because my feelings towards that part of myself are always conflicted. I have heard survivors of abuse say they hate the child they once were, the version of themselves which allowed the abuse to happen. But that does not describe me at all. I never hated her.

I pitied her.

And pity, I have come to understand, is not a good thing.

Pity is a dangerous, damaging emotion, because it demeans and belittles. Someone who is the object of pity is not a proud, dynamic force. And that is what I want to be.

So I have taken that injured child and I have placed her next to my heart. I want her to live there because that is where we can best have an emotional dialogue. I now know she has strengths and abilities I have not always acknowledged. I can learn from her, if I listen closely. She has, through pain and resilience, developed wisdom about the darkness that we all hold inside. It is important that we are aware it is there, because it will consume you, if you are not careful.

I lived in that darkness for a long while – it was there with me during my time in the north and it was always at the edge of my awareness during the worst part of my teens. It visited me in my dreams with visions of horror and it made me frightened of the shadows and the night. I will not let it have me again, and I know this damaged girl can protect me from it.

Keeping her close means I take better care of myself, too. Sometimes I feel her becoming anxious or upset by the little humps and bumps along life's road, and when that happens I know that I must take some time out to soothe her. I go somewhere quiet for a cup of tea, or I take a walk somewhere beautiful or, best of all, I go for a solitary run. She loves the air and the trees and the birdsong – she is a part of me, after all.

Because she is a child, she helps me grapple with my doubts about my parenting. I check in with her when I have a decision to make that I am struggling with, and she can indicate whether I am being fair or not – as a teenager, she has a finely tuned sense of what is fair and what is unfair. I value her opinions, because I know mine are often so skewed.

I'm not saying I've got it right, yet, but having her close by certainly helps.

The other thing that integrating this new part of myself has done is help me to regain something that I know was sorely lacking for a very long time – my sense of fun. Being attuned to my inner child means I am always ready now to laugh and sing and play and simply express joy. I have come to know that those parts of life which are joyful – the simple, honest pleasures each day gifts us with if we are open enough to see them and accept them – never went away. They were always there, but those shadows I have spent my life running from had clouded my vision so much I had become blind to happiness.

Not anymore. When something strikes me as funny I laugh. When I want to cry out in exultation, I make my cry and sing out to the skies that I am glad to be alive. For far too long my very existence was something I endured. Now it is something I treasure.

That I had to travel through the darkness to learn that makes it all the sweeter.

Running Towards the Light

I do not get much sleep on the night before Colm's fifty-mile run.

He and I trace the route in detail, and I am appalled to discover that, in actuality, it is a little over fifty-four miles. I point out to my coach and friend that human beings are not built for this kind of punishment, but he shrugs it off.

'My family has lost more good people to cancer than I want to even think about,' he says calmly. 'If by suffering a bit of discomfort and losing the odd toenail I can do something to help others, then it's a small price.'

I see there is no point in trying to reason with him, so I just tell him to load up on carbs before going to bed and that I'll see him tomorrow.

A team follows him from the start (the risks a run like this present mean it is essential to have a crew on standby). He sets a good pace, a comfortable jog, and makes steady progress. Colm is a quiet man, and while I tend to talk and chatter constantly throughout my races, complaining loudly when I feel bad and whooping and celebrating when I get an endorphin rush, Colm just plods on, saying very little, focusing on a point in the middle distance only he can see.

Throughout the day I keep in contact with his girlfriend via Facebook, and I share and post every hour or so, making sure everyone is aware of this amazing thing being done by such a beautiful soul.

At the halfway point, Colm gets a bit wobbly (to remind you, he has already run more than a standard marathon) and his team makes him pause for a second to take a few mouthfuls of pasta. He swallows the offering and keeps going.

I join him a short distance outside Dungarvan. He has now done close to fifty miles, and as I see him coming over the brow of a hill, my heart weeps for him – he is almost broken and every step is an ordeal. My friend's body temperature has dropped to a dangerous level, and he has been bundled up with extra clothes and a woolly hat. Dehydration has made him light-sensitive so a pair of wrap-around sunglasses cover his eyes.

I am with a group of women Colm trained for the Couch to 5K, and as we see him coming, we all begin to cheer and jeer him.

'For heaven's sake, Colm, what kind of a pace do you call this? You'll never finish at this rate!'

'It's a good thing we happened to be here to help you over the line!'

'Are you quite warm enough? I've a thermal vest in my bag I can loan you.'

An exhausted smile spreads across his pallid face, and he reaches out a hand for us to high-five. I fall in beside him, as I promised I would.

I can see he has gone beyond what most of us believe is our level of endurance. Speech is almost beyond him, so I begin to chat quietly. 'Do you remember when I started out, and you would run along beside me and I would just cry?'

He throws his eyes at me and makes a weak nod.

'I didn't think I could even do a 5K run back then, but you believed in me.'

He is listening. He can't respond, but he's hearing.

'You chose to run with me on my first half-marathon, and when I told you I couldn't go on, you promised me I could and you gave me the strength to do it. You carried my water and you carried all the extra clothes I'd brought – all my fucking baggage – and because you believed in me, I believed in myself.'

He looks at me then.

'You believed in me when I couldn't. You carried me when I was ready to give up. I'm here with you now, Colm. I know you're in pain and I know the end looks very far away, but look: you've got all these women running with you, and we're going to do it together.'

'Don't you know behind every great man is a great woman!'

This last comment is from a lady called Rose, who has only been running with us a short time. She is in her fifties and has never done more than 5K. At the sound of her voice, Colm turns painfully around.

'Rose,' he croaks. 'Are you there?'

'I'm here, Colm,' she calls.

'They're all here for you,' I tell him. 'They've all come out because you made their lives better and they want to help you do this crazy thing you've your heart set on.'

He grins through the agony and plods on.

At the grotto before Ballymacarbery, Colm wants to break into a sprint. He has amazing speed when he hits the accelerator, but I urge him to hold back.

'You want to finish strong,' I tell him. 'If you take off now, you might burn out and I want you running over that line, not crawling.'

He nods – he knows I'm right.

As we start up the final hill approaching the community centre, he begins to peel off the layers, and this time, I take them. He passes me the scarves and the sweatshirts and the hat and I accept them.

When I was at my darkest, he shouldered my burden. It is my turn to carry his for a while.

As we get near the village, we can hear the music and the cheers of his supporters.

'Your family are waiting for you,' I tell him. 'You're almost home.'

He looks at me with eyes filled with pain, exhaustion and hope.

'Go for it!' I tell him, and he breaks into that sprint.

Kids from the local school are spread across the road to make a human finish line, and they part as he barrels through them.

Colm started in Carriganore at 9.30 a.m. and he arrived back in Ballymacarbery at 7.00 p.m. He lost three toenails and had blisters on his feet the size of tennis balls.

And he raised €9,386 for cancer research.

Three days after the race I receive a text message from him: *I'm going on my first post ultra-marathon run. Fancy joining me?*

It is a beautiful afternoon as I get out of my car at the community centre where it all began. Colm is there, looking like he could do with a bit of feeding up, but he is grinning and stretching, and I know he is itching to go. Together, we turn out the gate and head down the lane towards the mountains.

Above the treeline, the sun is beaming. It feels warm on my face and the birds are singing and I am with my friend and, for the first time in a long time, the world seems like a friendly place.

'Do you fancy doing 10K?' Colm asks.

'Well, I don't have any other plans,' I say.

He laughs and we both break into a full-tilt explosion of speed.

All about me is light.

I am free.

Stephanie's Victim
Impact Statement

Today I would like to tell you a little bit of what you, Batty Prendergast, have inflicted on me throughout my life, of being raped and sexually abused repeatedly from my childhood through to my teenage years.

The pain I have carried silently growing up you will never know. You took from me everything a child should have as they grow up, while I was supposed to be protected by adults whose care I was in during this time.

I lost my virginity because of you and I wasn't even old enough to understand what you were taking from me. For this I will never ever forgive you.

The fear you put in me of never wanting it to get dark at

night time, the fear of going to bed never wanting to go to sleep in case you came to the room as you always did and cause me more pain and fear that I couldn't stop it.

I also hated having to take journeys alone with you in your lorry or van as I knew this always meant I would have to perform all these despicable acts that I hated and feared. I had to watch you full of pleasure and make me feel that this was normal, this was good.

When all these rape and sexual abuses took place, I would feel like I was going to die, I would feel as if I was choking and could not breathe; the fear was and will forever be inside me. This is all down to you; again, for this, I can never forgive you in my lifetime.

My life has been built around shame, regret, no confidence and hating myself, my body and everything about myself. I have missed out on so much happiness as a child, through to teenage years. You have robbed me of it all, my body can never heal or recover; you took it all for your pleasure but I will forever be paying the price for an evil, sick man.

I am every day fighting a battle to love my body, myself and feel beautiful inside and out. But I can't because of the dirty acts of abuse you inflicted on me.

In school and work I have never reached my full potential as my confidence and self-esteem is so low. This makes it a daily battle to hold down a job.

I deserve to be happy and believe in myself that I am beautiful inside and out because you made me feel dirty all my life and I blamed myself for not trying to stop you, but

I was just a child trusting that what you were doing to me was OK as you always reassured me it was OK.

I was led to believe by a family friend, a priest, that, in the eighties, you were fixed. Who fixed you? Was it the Catholic Church or HSE? I was told that there was proof of this, or so my sister, your wife, told me just under three years ago. If you were supposedly fixed, why did you continue to abuse me for years after? For this I feel very hurt, and let down by whoever fixed you I need answers from whom you spoke to help you at this time and again why as child I wasn't protected. This hurt goes on.

I went into a marriage that should have been a happy-ever-after time of my life but this wasn't to be as again my lack confidence and self-worth didn't allow me to stand up for myself and believe I deserved respect and love as again my past life was haunting me.

I have four beautiful children and I am so proud to be their mother, but they too have suffered because of you. Watching their mam going through depression, anxiety and lots of sadness. But they believe in me and know I would never let them down. In bringing this case to where I am today they have always had my back but they didn't deserve the pain you've inflicted on their mother; for this, again, I have no forgiveness.

I hope with the ongoing support of my partner Angelo, my children, my sister Deirdre and brothers Richie and Michael and their families I will start to find some peace and strength to begin a life I never knew I could have. I know I will never get back my beautiful, innocent, carefree childhood years but I can start to believe I was not wrong. I didn't ask for any of this torture. I will try to stop blaming myself for what you, you monster, inflicted on me; I am no longer your victim, I have taken back my life. I will never get my past back but now I have a future; you now will be the lonely one, with no friends, no voice, no independence. It was my voice and my sister's that you controlled and manipulated for many years but we are survivors.

You came into our family and broke our family home and chain forever, this can and will not ever be fixed. You, Batty Prendergast, you caused this the lives you have destroyed, it will forever be unforgiving.

I want you to fear sleep and fear being alone; I want you to forever more feel pain albeit with this you will just feel a little bit of my pain. I believe you should have done the right thing years ago and not put me through all I have suffered, and family members thinking I was making it up and causing me untold pain and suffering, that I didn't deserve.

You were in control of this all the time. My parents deserved better than to suffer because of your dirty work, you have broken them forever. The lives you have caused pain, suffering and grief to I will never forgive you. The scars, hurt and shame I have carried will live with me forever. No justice will ever let me forgive you.

I hope some day to be able to talk to other young girls going through similar abuse and that one day my sad, regretful, dirty, hurt feeling inside will do good for others to come forward and believe in themselves that they are not the ones to blame, it's the monsters that inflict such abuse and trauma on children.

I would like to thank An Garda Síochána for helping me throughout this case. Garda Clare Courtney, my liaison officer, who kept me strong and kept me believing in myself; Clare, you were always only a phone call away and this kind of support is so vital to victims. On my darkest days you helped me to go on, for this I am so grateful. Clare, I thank you from the bottom of my heart for being part of this terrible journey over the past three years.

I look at the family that have supported me unconditionally over the years and for always being by my side, today a little bit of justice has been given, so today is our day to have joy and relief. We have been waiting for this day with so many years, over the pain and suffering this monster Batty Prendergast has inflicted on us all as a family.

When I started this process the stress and anxiety was made so much worse than I could ever have imagined. But from today I will allow myself to believe in me and stop blaming myself for what I know was not my fault. My pain was caused by a monster that will never hurt me or anyone again.

Now it's time to see happiness and good times ahead for my children and partner. Today I take my life back. I am so glad to get this day to be able to stand here in front of my family and friends and say what I've wanted to say for years to you, Batty Prendergast. I have won, I have survived, and now my life starts and yours ends lonely and miserable, which is just what you deserve. You can never hurt anyone again; from this I take great peace.

I hope by going public today I can help other victims going through what I have and still am, that it will help them to come forward and believe they too have a voice and are not to blame.

Finally, you, Batty Prendergast, you have been protected for long enough; now people will see the real you and the hurt, pain, shame and fear you instilled in us throughout the years while in your presence. I will never forgive you.

Stephanie Hickey
July 30th 2018

Acknowledgements

This book is for my children. Without them, life would have been very different for me – in truth, my life would probably have ended a long time ago. I also want to dedicate my story to Angelo, who stuck by me even when I tried to push him away. There were a lot of years when I simply didn't know how to be in a relationship, but he never gave up on me. He never gave up on us.

Having my nephew Colm Geary behind me was critical. He was insistent that it didn't matter how many years passed, I had to go to the guards and have my voice heard. Having him behind me was critical. He was a very big part of my life during the dark years, when I was living alone and every day was a struggle.

My sister Deirdre and her husband Ciaran always

reassured me I was doing the right thing. As I hope this book demonstrates, Deedee has been my rock. My brothers Richie and Michael and their wives and families supported me through the trial, and it would not be an exaggeration to say I couldn't have done it without them.

And I must say a word about my parents. It is a constant source of pain for me that my father has passed and didn't get to see this book published. I am in no doubt that his and my mother's strength as parents and the upbringing I got is the source of whatever small courage I possess. They raised their children in hard times, but we never felt we missed out on anything.

The Victim Support at Court service (V-SAC), which is a voluntary agency, made my experience in the Central Criminal Court bearable. They dealt with me and Deedee with care, love and sensitivity, and I don't think their work gets the recognition it deserves. They are truly amazing people.

I would like to thank the close friends who supported me through the trial and those who travelled to Dublin to stand with me.

Lastly, I want to thank Shane Dunphy. In him I have made a friend for life: I could not have written this book with anyone else. From the first day I met Shane I felt safe and reassured that this was the person to bring my story out into the light. Shane has a beautiful sense of warmth and calmness, and he instinctively 'got' me and what I have been through. I felt he saw the real me, and through the many conversations we had in the process of writing he taught me something important that I want to share with other survivors.

When people say it's over and that you should move on, remember that what happened happened – it is wrong and it shouldn't have, but it did, and is part of your personal history. It will never go away (all the goodwill in the world can't make it unhappen), but to survive you must reorganise your life and your sense of self around it. The hurt and pain you experienced don't define you and they don't alter your true self. They just become a part of it.

The real power we can have as survivors is to no longer allow the pain to dominate our lives – but to acknowledge that we were hurt, to confront that experience and to set it aside.

I have taken so much from that.

Shane taught me that it's OK to have bad days, days when I don't want to get up. He helped me to see that I am allowed to have those days, and I don't need to beat myself up for having them. Deciding that, today, I'm going to close the door and just have some 'me' time is a kind of self-care. A kind of self love.

And there are days when I smile and chat and put on a show for the world, but that's what it is: a show. And that's OK too.

Because I am learning to love myself again. And that has been the greatest gift this journey has bestowed upon me.